THE DEVIL AND UNCLE SAM

A Foreign Policy Research Institute Book

This book is sponsored by the Foreign Policy Research Institute in Philadelphia. Founded in 1955, the Institute is an independent, nonprofit organization devoted to research on issues affecting the national interest of the United States.

THE DEVIL AND UNCLE SAM

A User's Guide to the Friendly Tyrants Dilemma

Adam Garfinkle

Kenneth Adelman
Patrick Clawson
Mark Falcoff
Douglas J. Feith
Daniel Pipes

Transaction Publishers
New Brunswick (U.S.A.) and London (U.K.)

Copyright © 1992 by Transaction Publishers, New Brunswick, New Jersey
08903

All rights reserved under International and Pan-American Copyright
Conventions. No part of this book may be reproduced or transmitted in any
form or by any means, electronic or mechanical, including photocopy,
recording, or any information storage and retrieval system, without prior
permission in writing from the publisher. All inquiries should be addressed
to Transaction Publishers, Rutgers–The State University, New Brunswick,
New Jersey 08903.

Library of Congress Catalog Number: 91-32579
ISBN: 1-56000-012-0
Printed in the United States of America

Library of Congress Cataloging-in-Publication Data

The devil and Uncle Sam: a user's guide to the friendly tyrants
dilemma/Adam Garfinkle . . . [et al.].
   p.   cm.
   Includes index.
   ISBN 1-56000-012-0
   1. United States–Foreign relations–1945-1989. 2. Authoritarianism. 3.
Despotism. 4. Human rights. 5. World politics–1945– I. Garfinkle, Adam
M., 1951–
327.73–dc20   91–32579
                                           CIP

Contents

Preface

For more than forty years, the U.S. government has struggled with the challenge of maintaining useful relations with a special breed of regime: those whose rulers profess a community of interests with the United States and, at the same time, rule through authoritarian means. Relationships with such rulers — who for purposes of both intellectual provocation and concision we call Friendly Tyrants — almost invariably generate tensions between the need to pursue prudent security strategies and the ideal of promoting liberty and human rights worldwide. And even when such tensions are well managed, the weakening and collapse of Friendly Tyrants' governments invariably afflict U.S. foreign policy with crises of varying intensities and durations.

Such tensions and crises have bedeviled American policy since the founding of the Republic, but they have been especially intense between those days when Harry S. Truman sat in the White House and our own — that is, during the cold war. Yet despite the recurring problems posed by Friendly Tyrants over the past forty-five years, little effort has been made to understand these relationships and their crises in a systematic way. Given Washington's rather mixed track record over the years, we thought a comparative study would prove interesting and useful. It was interesting, and this little volume is our attempt to make it useful, for even in a post-cold war environment, the Friendly Tyrants problem is still with us, as the heated arguments over the propriety and wisdom of coming to the aid of Kuwait and Saudi Arabia after August 2, 1990, illustrate.

Three years of inquiry into this subject by scholars and former policy makers produced the detailed scholarly study edited by Daniel Pipes and myself, *Friendly Tyrants: An American Dilemma*, published by St. Martin's Press in 1991. Much of the counsel we offer here derives from that volume. This *User's Guide* distills the results of that effort not for scholars, but for those actually on the firing line today, be they in the executive branch, the Congress, the media, or business.

To produce this *User's Guide*, we assembled a team of authors with diverse talents and experience:

Kenneth Adelman, director of the Arms Control and Disarmament Agency from 1982-87;

Patrick Clawson, an economist for many years with the World Bank, and presently a research associate at the Foreign Policy Research Institute;

Mark Falcoff of the American Enterprise Institute, a former staff member of the Senate Foreign Relations Committee;

Douglas J. Feith, a deputy assistant secretary of defense from 1984-86, a member of the National Security Council staff from 1981-82, and presently a cofounder and partner in the Washington law firm of Feith and Zell;

Daniel Pipes, director of the Foreign Policy Research Institute and a former State Department hand; and

Adam Garfinkle, chair of the Authors' Committee and coordinator of the political studies program at the Foreign Policy Research Institute.

Every author contributed directly to the repeated rewriting and reorganizing of the text so that, in the form we present it here, it is truly a single work of many hands.

When we finished our work, we sought a group of highly experienced senior reviewers to criticize what we had done:

Richard L. Armitage, who is at this writing managing both U.S.-Philippine basing negotiations and water negotiations between Jordan and Israel, is one of America's most experienced diplomats. As an assistant secretary of defense in the Reagan administration, he was an integral part of the team that managed the Philippine crisis of 1986.

Stephen W. Bosworth, currently head of the U.S.-Japan Foundation, was U.S. ambassador to the Philippines during the 1986 crisis.

Frank C. Carlucci was U.S. ambassador to Portugal during its Friendly Tyrants crisis in 1974. He was also secretary of defense from 1987-89.

Ambler Moss, Jr., among his many diplomatic assignments, was U.S. ambassador to Panama during a time when General Manuel Noriega was still our friend.

Joseph J. Sisco has served an an assistant secretary of state and as under secretary of state, and has undertaken innumerable special assignments all over the world in the course of his diplomatic career.

Robert Strausz-Hupé, the founder of the Foreign Policy Research Institute, is one America's most distinguished diplomats, having served as U.S. ambassador to Sri Lanka, Sweden, Belgium, NATO, and, most recently, Turkey.

To our delight, our reviewers liked what we had done. But they criticized it, too, and we took their suggestions to heart. All of them generously devoted considerable time to helping us refine our work, and we thank them all very deeply for it. They are not, however, responsible for any errors of fact or interpretation that may remain in the pages ahead.

Understanding the patterns of the past does not yield a set formula for policy makers in the future, but it does offer insights that should prove superior to relying on intuition in times of stress. And certainly it is not too late to learn, for there will be more Friendly Tyrants crises in our future. They will have unique features, to be sure, but they will also have features in common with crises past. The unique features may cause new mistakes to be made, and such mistakes can be forgiven. It is unforgivable, however, to make old mistakes all over again. This *User's Guide* aims at helping to prevent the preventable.

The obstinate ambiguities that attend political life, however, make it impossible to offer simple solutions to the hellishly messy problems that attend America's relations with Friendly Tyrants. But we have tried our best at least to organize this complexity so that what follows below can serve policy makers. Thus, we offer the results of our study in the form of ten maxims, each one broken down into component precepts. Each of these precepts begins with a general principle or explanation, then goes on to give examples of it. When appropriate, we have tried to spice up some of our points with humor.

Before presenting the maxims and their precepts, however, a few words about the Friendly Tyrants dilemma itself, and why it matters.

Adam Garfinkle

Introduction:
The Friendly Tyrants Dilemma

The United States has been dealing with pro-American, or at least anti-communist, authoritarian regimes for as long as the United States has been a great power. These dealings have generally been justified as both necessary and lesser evils: necessary because only a minority of countries are democracies, and great powers cannot afford to ignore the majority that are not; and lesser because such relationships have been seen, at least until quite recently, as a means to contain the direct expansion of Soviet power and of movements ideologically sympathetic to it. Being able to distinguish between lesser and greater evils is a sign of moral sophistication, for whoever ignores the existence of varying degrees of evil is bound eventually to become a servant of evil.

But evils are still evils, even if they are necessary and lesser ones. On occasion, it is true, Americans and their government have managed to live with an authoritarian ally for many years without special discomfort; ties with Franco's Spain over more than three decades come to mind, as does the current relationship with the Indonesian regime of General Suharto. More often, however, such relationships eventually degenerate into crisis that jeopardize U.S. interests. Just recalling the names of a few rulers — Batista of Cuba, Trujillo of the Dominican Republic, Diem of South Vietnam, Mohammed Reza Pahlavi of Iran, Somoza of Nicaragua, the Duvaliers of Haiti, Marcos of the Philippines — gives new meaning to the aphorism that with certain friends, one has no need for enemies.

The Friendly Tyrants dilemma encompasses more than a series of disconnected events, however. It arises from the characteristic style and basic circumstances of postwar American foreign policy. Patterns emerge from a systematic, comparative review of the Friendly Tyrants experience, even though Friendly Tyrants' regimes differ. Some of those patterns concern the warnings of political weakness and incipient crisis. Others have more to do with the characteristic pattern of American responses to Friendly Tyrants and their crises.

Some patterns are obvious; for example, the narrower the social and political base of the tyrant, the more likely his regime is to fail rapidly and totally. Others are counterintuitive: it turns out that the more important a country is to the United States, the harder it is for the U.S. government to formulate a coherent policy. Many, perhaps most, of the patterns discussed below are neither very obvious nor very surprising, but illustrate instead the rich complexity that comes from a detailed study of political life and the policy-making process.

The Friendly Tyrants problem is not about to go away, despite the end of the cold war. Many nondemocratic states with sound relationships with the United States are still around — Zaire, Indonesia, Morocco, Saudi Arabia, and Mexico come most easily to mind — and a number of new, weak, partial, or fragile democracies in the world today will no doubt result in a new crop of potential Friendly Tyrants crises in the future — South Korea, Taiwan, Thailand, Kenya, Pakistan, Brazil, Argentina, Guatemala, El Salvador, Panama, and Peru come to mind. Thus, questions asked in the past — how to balance U.S. strategic interests with the promotion of human rights, how to get close enough to a dictator to influence him, but not so close as to be tarred by his misdeeds, and many others besides — are likely to be asked again in the future. It would be nice to know, would it not, with what general level of intelligence and success these questions have been handled up until now?

So, for example, in Latin America, what was the United States to do with anticommunist but undemocratic rulers like Augusto Pinochet of Chile, or Alfredo Stroessner of Paraguay? Should Washington have rewarded these regimes for their anti-Soviet policies or punished them for their undemocratic misdeeds at home? In Asia, the same questions arose over the Rhee regime in South Korea and the Diem regime in South Vietnam. They are with us today with regard to General Suharto in Indonesia, and the military junta in Thailand. Is it best to treat them gently because of their useful strategic roles, or to pressure them because of their domestic shortcomings? In Africa, how well did Washington do with Samuel Doe's crisis in Liberia, or Siad Barre's in Somalia? How should it handle Mobutu Sese Seko in Zaire, or the South African apartheid regime today? In the Middle East, what about King Hasan of Morocco, the House of Saud in Arabia, the returned al-Sabah dynasty in Kuwait, or President Zine El Abidine Ben Ali of Tunisia?

Obviously, not all Friendly Tyrants are alike; some are friendlier than others, and some are clearly more tyrannical than others. To repeat, the label "Friendly Tyrants" is a moniker, not an analytical term. According to the dictionary meaning of the word, a tyrant is someone whose rule transgresses in barbarity and cruelty even the standards of his own time and place. A tyrant is a ruler who harms his own society and people, and the word implies pathological behavior in high places. Therefore, it isn't entirely fair to lump together true tyrants like the barbarous junta of Greek colonels that ruled in Athens in the 1967-1974 period, with, say, mild-mannered monarchs like King Hasan of Morocco who rules a traditional society and who, like King Hussein of Jordan and President Hosni Mubarak of Egypt, is cautiously opening up his country's political processes. The Argentine junta of the late 1970s and early 1980s was brutal, harsh, and oppressive in ways that Mexico's long-lived corporatist authoritarianism simply is not.

Moreover, the trajectory of political decency in some Friendly Tyrannies is upward, in others downward. Both Taiwan and South Korea are rapidly modernizing societies; they are full-blown success stories from a U.S. foreign policy perspective because in contrast to their kindred communist neighbors — the People's Republic of China and North Korea — they are prosperous, secure, and increasingly pluralistic political cultures. In other cases, like El Salvador and Guatemala, progress is much slower and more fragile. And Zaire is not headed on an upward course at all. Over some Friendly Tyrants, too, there have been arguments about the direction of change, like South Vietnam in the past, and South Africa today.

Relatedly, some authoritarian regimes are historical aberrations, like Greece under the junta. But others are tediously normal — as in Saudi Arabia. Where pluralist political systems have been sustained, authoritarian regimes tend to be tenuous, as Turkey's three brief episodes of military rule since 1960 illustrate. In contrast, the political cultures of Zaire and Iran show that authoritarianism can have deep roots.

Finally, some dictatorships are personalistic and these are usually the most prone to sudden crisis — like Samuel Doe's in Liberia. More institutionalized regimes are less likely to unravel quickly — like Pinochet's in Chile. Fully corporatist ones are more stable yet; the power of the PRI (Partido Revolucionario Institucional) in Mexico and the white South African regime are examples. In personalistic dictatorships, the regime changes dramatically when personalities change; in corporatist dictatorships, it usually does not.

But despite all of these differences, Friendly Tyrants are all the same in at least one way: most Americans feel at least some misgivings about a close U.S. association with them. Many rule through military govern-ments and so arouse an instinctive American distaste. Even those regimes that are not martial lack real enthusiasm for accountable government, distort the rule of law, and abrogate basic human rights. They frequently depend on violence, glorify militarism, and display the ugly arrogance of authoritarianism.

Further, there are practical reasons for worrying about Friendly Tyrants. As with Panama's Manuel Noriega, their policies can change with a whistle and a whim, making their friendliness undependable. Even when friendliness does endure, as with the shah of Iran, the regime may not.

At the same time, most Americans understand that good relations with these leaders can serve U.S. objectives, and thereby the cause of freedom. Friendly Tyrants often have joined efforts to contain Moscow and its proxies. More recently in the Persian Gulf war, Friendly Tyrants in Egypt, Saudi Arabia, Morocco (and, temporarily, even Syria!) helped the United States defeat Iraqi evil on the march. Friendly Tyrants may occupy strategic positions or contain vital resources. Whatever the faults of Friendly Tyrants, they are often less egregious than those of other regimes in the region. And as Ayatollah Khomeini and the Sandinista regime showed so dramatically, alternative rulers may be even worse than those already in power for their own people as well as for American interests.

What, then, is the proper nature of American ties with such countries? How horrible does a government have to be before we foreswear cooperation with it? How important must a security interest be that we are willing to deal with not only the good, but also the bad and the ugly? If the regime becomes worse or American interests become less impor-tant, at what point, if any, does it make sense to withdraw support, and even to collaborate in the overthrow of a Friendly Tyrant?

Basic Choices

Extreme cases create the easiest consensus. When in dire straits, the U.S. government, like all others, will do what it must to survive. In the War of Independence, Americans allied with Louis XVI of France, a proponent of the divine right of kings, against the far more liberal King George III. In World War II, it was fairly easy to make common cause with Stalin against the Axis; the whole world was at stake and Nazism was clearly the greater evil. At the other extreme, nothing would bring

Americans to embrace the likes of Jean Bédel Bokassa or Idi Amin, horrid rulers of strategically marginal countries.

Most occasions for decision are less dramatic and are instead bounded by conflicting pressures. In normal times, the U.S. government finds it impossible to have untroubled relations with South Africa or to go on calmly with business as usual with China after the massacre at Tiananmen Square. But no U.S. administration is prepared to abandon states as crucial to U.S. interests as these, either. Nor in the past has any U.S. administration treated strategically important countries like Iran or the Philippines the same way as less significant ones like Haiti or Nicaragua.

The difficulties in dealing with Friendly Tyrants exist at two overlapping levels: the ideological and the pragmatic. The ideological level concerns values — what is right and wrong. The pragmatic level concerns efficacy — what works and what does not. These levels are clearly connected, for there is nothing to be gained by knowing what is right but not how to achieve it.

Realism and Idealism

Ideas matter; they establish the milieu in which policy is made and define its possibilities. Values matter, too; they provide much of the energy that drives democratic politics. The Friendly Tyrants dilemma never seems to go away for long because it raises a question of basic values: what kind of country do Americans wish the United States to be? Should it be a great power in the traditional manner, or a great power that carries great moral force? Is the goal of American diplomacy to further state interests or to redeem the world? Americans would like to have it both ways, of course, and in truth these aims are not always mutually exclusive. But sometimes they are, and then the real question is: When the two desiderata conflict, which takes priority? Friendly Tyrants crises highlight this dilemma with special clarity.

The dilemma stems from the tension between an austere geostrategic calculus of American influence and an exuberant moral vision of America's unique goodness — between realism (or realpolitik) and idealism. When it comes to Friendly Tyrants, realists see no choice but for the U.S. government to find its friends wherever it can in order to serve the national interest and preserve the world's brightest beacon of freedom. Relations with Friendly Tyrants are a means that is justified by the end. A few observers go further, voicing an outright preference for authoritarian allies on the premise that they are easier to deal with than democratic ones.[1] Idealists are troubled by U.S. friendliness toward authoritarian regimes not only because of the nasty taste it leaves, but because they believe it undermines the practical power of the American example and unnecessarily creates enemies.[2] Befriending tyrannies, idealists argue, confuses short term expediency for the real national interest.

Realpolitik is found all over the world; the pervasive idealistic strain in American politics, however, makes this country's foreign policy distinctive. Idealism goes back to the nation's founding by the religious pilgrims and pioneers who endowed American public life with its uniquely moral tone. The luxury of relative isolation and power, too, allowed Americans to nurture a self-image of their country as a new Jerusalem, a city on the hill blessedly detached from the corrupt power politics of a decrepit Europe — this was and has remained the essence of American exceptionalism. The absence of a nationalism steeped in a myth of ancient bloodlines contributed to the development of a highly abstract national vision at the center of which stood the moral consensus of the day. Most other states can endure whatever their form of government may be;[3] but America cannot be imagined except as a constitutional system of government. For other states, even those (like Sweden and India) that imbue public diplomacy with moralism, the bedrock of national security remains physical protection of the homeland; for America, it also includes a way of life. That is why the adjective "un-American" has few, if any, real parallels elsewhere.

Tension between realism and idealism pervades American history from the beginning, as even a cursory comparison of Jefferson and Hamilton, or Madison and Washington, would show. The issues differ, but precursors of the Friendly Tyrants problem can be found in arguments between New England transcendentalists and the warriors of manifest destiny in the 1840s, between Mugwumps and jingo-imperialists in the 1890s, and between isolationists and Wilsonian internationalists during and after World War I. Although obscured temporarily during that exceptional era of consensus that lasted from roughly 1942 to about 1966, this tension has since returned to center stage.

Since the denouement of the Vietnam War, American foreign policy has migrated back to its older moral perspective (though, for some, with a novel ideological twist bequeathed by the New Left). Contemporary isolationists, like those of old, are skeptical of foreign entanglements; internationalists see no alternative to active American policies in the world. The battle lines are not so clear these days, however, for there are liberal and conservative forms of both isolationism and interventionism.

This said, most conservatives would sacrifice less in the way of security interests, and so tend to be viewed as the realists. Most liberals would sacrifice less in the way of democratic values, and so tend to be seen as the idealists.

As ever, each of these groups sees itself as having the exactly appropriate mix of realism and idealism. Neither claim is outlandish: no matter how realpolitik-minded, every American accepts the role of scruples in public policy at some level; and every idealist accepts that national interests have some place in his deliberations.

What really separates the two approaches comes out most clearly in their attitudes to policy options. Realists and idealists subject policy options to different kinds of tests. An idealist is likely to ask early on whether a proposed action conforms to international law; for a realpolitiker, such a question would be low on the list, if it is there at all. Similarly, the idealist takes seriously the potential negative reactions and possible help to be obtained through multilateral forums such as the United Nations and the Organization of American States, while the realist tends to see these organizations as a nuisance. The realist takes seriously the projection of resolve and willpower; to the idealist, such considerations are often seen as macho self-entrapments.

But the most basic difference of opinion concerns the use of force and covert operations. The realist instinctively considers all available instruments of state, including force and covert operations, in proportion to the risk to interests at stake. Idealists tend to consider such instrumentalities only as a last resort. Thus, Secretary of State Cyrus Vance opposed the 1980 attempt to rescue American hostages in Iran, and resigned his office over it, because he believed that a diplomatic solution might still be possible, and that it was therefore premature to repair to the last resort. Some idealists rule out dissimulation and force even as a last resort, in the belief that their use is always counterproductive.[4] That's why most foreign policy idealists wanted to give economic sanctions years to work before using force against Iraq in 1991, and most realists did not.

These lines are not hard and fast, of course. Most realists opposed the use of force in Panama from the time of the U.S. indictment against General Manuel Noriega in February 1988 and over the next year and a half, because they saw the threats to American interests as insufficient to warrant the risk. Conversely, some idealists, usually opposed to military intervention, favored it to restore the democratic process in Panama. Also, idealists have been more enthusiastic than realists about using U.S. armed forces to restrict the flow of drugs from South America.

As lines of ideological engagement blur, American responses to Friendly Tyrants have become unsystematic. It is more accurate to speak of tendencies rather than ideologies and, as a result, the particularities of each case as it comes along — the personalities, the media patina of the day, the state of U.S. domestic politics, the administration's reputation — tend to drive perceptions and policies. This condition affects not only the debate about values, but policy choices, too.

When to Fix the Roof?

At the policy level, the key dilemma has less to do with philosophical approach than with timing. Although there are notable exceptions, most authoritarian regimes are notoriously unstable; even those that last a long time fail to provide for a smooth, nonviolent transition. The problem of dealing with dictators would remain in the moral realm alone were it not for this troublesome reality. The practical problem comes in the form of a damned if you do, damned if you don't dilemma. If you push a tyrant hard to reform, you may destabilize him and get something worse for the effort — like Castro and the Sandinistas, for instance, who almost made Batista and Somoza look good by comparison. But if you don't push for reform, the tyrant will in time destabilize himself, and you will often reap the whirlwind when he does — as with the shah of Iran and the Greek junta.

The problem facing the U.S. government can be illuminated by the parable of the man living in a house with a leaky roof. A visitor asks the man why he does not fix the roof. "Because I cannot fix the leak when it is raining," he answers, "and when it is not raining, there is no leak."

This is not mere facetiousness. A crisis is no time to push a Friendly Tyrant toward reform; it is too late for basic maintenance and, since to patch a hole properly usually requires that it first be widened, one risks a deluge by trying. But when there is no crisis, there is little pressure to act and, in the past, Washington has often learned to overlook the sins of Friendly Tyrants in the interests of untroubled relations.

Implicit in this choice is a calculus (better to accept longer-term risks for shorter-term gains) and a plan (change course only when risks outweigh benefits). This approach has obvious attractions for an administration whose term lasts only four years, but it has costs, too. With time, the consciousness of a trade-off grows dim, while bureaucratic routine erodes intellectual vigilance. Almost imperceptibly, the tyrants' interests become our interests, their crises become our crises, and their failures become our failures.

Changing course becomes ever harder as time passes. Policy makers and others outside the government may occasionally become anxious over undiminished American support for a Friendly Tyrant in changing circumstances, but creating a consensus to disturb the relationship is well nigh impossible. This is especially so with respect to large countries bearing important U.S. interests. There is always someone to argue that risking a tyrant's enmity or collapse exceeds any likely benefit from U.S. pressure. And reforming or removing a Friendly Tyrant is so hard to pull off successfully that a strategy for living with the dictator often makes sense. Thus, the counsel of caution is almost sure to win a decisive following most of the time.

Most of the time, but not always. On occasion, the U.S. government has tried to fix the roof by demanding reform or, failing that, by removing a Friendly Tyrant — in both cases hoping to head off future disaster. The option of reform is extremely important: it is essential to give Friendly Tyrants an alternative between just staying or leaving, to point the way to actions they can take that would relieve U.S. pressure on them.

Even so, the results of such pressures have been very mixed. The U.S. effort to promote reform in Iran in the early 1960s was an example of repair work left unfinished. Ferdinand Marcos, for example, always had the option of making the necessary reforms. That he did not avail himself of this option points up the difficulties of persuading Friendly Tyrants to change. And while Marcos's removal from the Philippines in 1986 worked well, usually the repair job is so tardy or so badly done that it destroys the house, as in the cases of Diem, Batista, and Somoza. Even when the U.S. presence has appeared overwhelming and where Washington has acted before the critical crisis point, controlling the collapse of one regime and easing the transition to another has proven to be extraordinarily difficult.

One reason that it is so hard to manage transitions from crisis to a new stability is that as a Friendly Tyrants episode unfolds, it often becomes politically domesticated. In part, this is because raising the visibility of an issue raises the bureaucratic stakes and expands the number of actors involved. Raising the visibility of an issue and expanding the number of actors involved in a decision also have the effect of lowering the average level of information and sensitivity to the facts of a particular case. But that is the only way to handle important problems, and it is necessary that responsible officials who see a bigger picture than regional experts make key decisions. Still, as a result of how the decision-making process usually works, a recurrent theme of Friendly Tyrant crises revolves around problems of cooperation and coordination in the bureaucracy.

But there is more. The American way of making major foreign policy decisions is extraordinarily porous; in no other country do foreign policy experts both in and out of the government play such a small role and the public — via the Congress, the press, the lobbies, and occasional street demonstrations — play such a large one. Sometimes a Friendly Tyrants episode takes on the trappings of a political circus, and the porosity of the decision process becomes even more extreme. Issues extraneous to foreign policy take over, at the expense of foreign policy specialists, when a Friendly Tyrants crisis relates directly to some domestic concern like war (Vietnam), race relations (South Africa), or drugs (Panama).

In these cases, the debate usually takes on an especially sharp realist versus idealist quality. The executive branch and conservatives usually adopt the realist position, while Congress and liberals adopt the idealist one. A parallel debate also rages along a save-the-friend vs. dump-the-dictator axis. Formerly marginal and eccentric arguments made by lobbyists or intellectuals about the moral deficiencies of a regime become relevant, even persuasive.

Timing Is Everything

Ultimately, the fixing-the-roof problem boils down to a matter of timing. And here it is important to understand that it is not just American politics that create the Friendly Tyrants problem, but also the unpredictable vicissitudes of authoritarian regimes themselves. Not even the most extreme U.S. maladroitness can create a Friendly Tyrants crisis without some help; a serious crisis takes at least two actors. The volatility of authoritarian regimes assures the permanence of the Friendly Tyrants dilemma, and even the occasional acute crisis. The American side of a Friendly Tyrants crisis goes through stages only because Friendly Tyrannies do too. The question, then, is not only what the U.S. government should do, but when it should do it.

The decay and collapse of authoritarian regimes usually determine the timing of a crisis and provide the personalities with whom the U.S. government must deal. Crises do not emerge overnight; they ripen. Becoming more aware of the ripening process means knowing in advance which Friendly Tyrants are headed toward collapse, which face important mid-term regime decisions, which might be saved from a further descent into authoritarianism. Knowing these things vastly improves the chances of dealing effectively with troubles of many sorts.

The life cycle of a Friendly Tyrant, therefore, defines discrete U.S. objectives. Thus, moving precipitously to pressure a Friendly

Tyrant to reform shows bad timing if it risks undermining a cooperative regime when it is not weak, and, from the U.S. point of view, the alternatives are worse. It is also bad timing to support a tyrant for so long that his final crisis so tars American interests that they fall with him.

The phases of a Friendly Tyranny can be described by analogy to the flight of a missile — boost, mid-course, and terminal. U.S. policies that might work during the boost phase of a Friendly Tyrant's cycle (restraint, pressure, support) could well be counterproductive later on. Policy must address the right questions at the right times, or it will probably be ineffective.

Boost. The best way to head off Friendly Tyrants crises is to help democracies from backsliding into authoritarianism, or to encourage authoritarian regimes toward political pluralism and accountability. This is harder to do than it is to say, but the effort must be made. Fragile democracies must be supported; not to do so is simply a bad investment in the future.

But what if democracy is not a near-term alternative? Is it better to urge a Friendly Tyranny to reform even if it cannot democratize? If so, how should the U.S. government promote reform; what leverage and which enticements should it use and which should it avoid? How fast should it move? When should it do nothing? What risks should it be prepared to run of alienating or undermining a friendly dictator, particularly if the most likely replacements are worse for the country and for U.S. interests?

Alternately, is it better for the U.S. government to accept the flaws of Friendly Tyrants, contenting itself with a useful but short relationship? If this is Washington's choice, it runs a greater risk of eventually playing into the hands of its enemies. The terminal crisis is likely to be that much worse, too. Therefore, ways must be sought — like insuring liaison with opposition groups — to look to the long term without undermining the regime. This is not easy to do.

Mid-course. In the mid-course of a Friendly Tyranny, certain telltale signs of decrepitude and regime weakness begin to emerge. Indeed, indicators of weakness and drift precede by many months the onset of nearly every acute regime crisis. The tyrant's inner circle divides among itself. Repression rises as the regime loses its grip. Corruption begins to exceed local standards of tolerance. Capital flees the country. The regime adopts a bellicose foreign policy. (Greek intrigues against Archbishop Makarios in Cyprus in 1974 and the Argentine assault on the Falklands in 1982 are classic examples of indulging in the habit of exporting domestic troubles through foreign military adventures.) Opposition groups, which had cooperated in hopes of a chance to overthrow the regime, fall out among themselves as power beckons, leading to more violence. Opposition groups on the left may turn to the Soviets or Chinese or Cubans for help (as did the Sandinistas), as other groups look to the United States (as occurred in Iran and in the Philippines).

Evocative appeals by opposition groups to American and international audiences can greatly complicate U.S. policy. If political struggle abroad is imported into the American debate, signals emanating from that debate, in turn, can have influence in the country. In the Nicaraguan case, the waning of U.S. support for Somoza enlarged and divided the opposition to him, in turn forcing U.S. policy to operate in a more complex and volatile environment. When the American patron is seen as hedging bets, a nervous tyrant usually reacts by growing more anxious, and therefore more bellicose. Somoza after 1977 exactly fit this pattern.

It is at the mid-course stage that a menu of structural reforms ought to be suggested, buttressed with offers of U.S. aid to see them through — before the regime's trouble leads it to become a dictatorial celebrity in the United States, with the lack of control over policy that this implies. Before the onset of trouble, the regime will wish to resist reform and will have the power and self-confidence to do so. After deterioration is advanced, reform may be impossible. Indeed, timing is everything.

Terminal. In the face of crisis, an administration must not appear cynical or passive, nor can it afford to panic. The proper balance is extremely difficult to achieve, especially as an administration convulsed by a Friendly Tyrants crisis must speak simultaneously to several different audiences, including American friends and opponents, the tyrant, the tyrant's anti-American opposition, the Soviet Union, and regional powers.

In the terminal stage, the essential questions that U.S. policy makers ask change. Is it better to cut a loss or stick with an ally so that other pro-American leaders feel reassured? When is it time to cut the line or to switch sides? Under what conditions should the U.S. government use direct force to protect a threatened regime (as it did in Vietnam and Kuwait)?

Distancing is clearly much harder in cases where the U.S. government has a long or an intimate involvement in the regime's day-to-day affairs. The U.S. role in Panama in 1988-89 is an example of a situation from which distancing was not an option. Clearly, too, effective distancing — the "decent interval" — was not possible in South Vietnam, but it was in Haiti and in Argentina under the junta. If Americans vouchsafe disproportionate interests in a Friendly Tyrants, the threat to U.S. interests in a tyrant's fall is partly a function of U.S. policy — the U.S. "suffocation" of the shah of Iran after 1969 is a case in point.

Timing usually determines whether things get completely or only partially out of control. No one saw what was about to hit the shah in time to do much about it, but astute decision makers in Washington saw the deterioration of the Marcos regime and acted in time to avert disaster.

Indeed, most striking of all in the Friendly Tyrants phenomenon is the pattern of extraordinarily rapid unravelling by a regime. At the end, the rebels found it surprisingly easy to push out Batista; the regimes of Baby Doc Duvalier, the Greek colonels, and the Argentine generals virtually fell of their own weight. This creates policy problems for the United States, however, because if predicting the end is hard, then so is managing it properly. Underestimate the speed of decline, and you are ill-prepared. Overestimate it, however, and you look foolish — as with Panama in March 1987 and again in October 1989.

When pressed, even the man with the leaky roof knows that eventually it will rain. Everybody else — including other U.S. allies and anti-American predators on the loose — knows it too. Knowing when to fix the roof, therefore, depends on being able to predict the weather and that, said Simon Dedalus in *Ulysses*, "is as uncertain as a child's bottom."

The Price of Failure

However hard it is to properly manage a Friendly Tyrants crisis, it is very important. Policy failures vis-à-vis Friendly Tyrants have resulted in serious setbacks for the United States. In the Caribbean, failure to control regime transitions after U.S. policy deliberately undermined two Friendly Tyrants resulted in the creation of a Soviet beachhead in Cuba and, until 1989, a potential second front in Nicaragua. Failure of a different sort in Greece between April 1967 and August 1973 earned Washington the lasting enmity of many Greeks. Failure in Vietnam undermined containment and bedeviled the formulation and implementation of American foreign policy for more than a decade. In Iran, it meant the loss of crucial intelligence posts and tracking stations and the rise to power of a very hostile regime, headed by Ayatollah Ruhollah Khomeini.

Failures in managing Friendly Tyrants crisis always lead to recriminations at home, too. Indeed, Friendly Tyrants episodes are the nub of some of the most visceral debates in postwar American foreign policy. They have also served as a reference point for waging battles over the next crisis, sometimes for many years.

Disagreement over U.S. policy in the Chinese civil war, for example, fueled McCarthyism and prefigured American commitments in Korea and Southeast Asia in the 1950s. The mishandling of Batista in 1958 influenced how the U.S. government chose to deal with Trujillo and Papa Doc Duvalier in the early 1960s. The Vietnam disaster was so traumatic that it arguably contributed to the collapse of two U.S. administrations and created a generation of officials scarred for life by failure and guilt. The neo-isolationism of this group goes far to explain the Carter administration's attitude toward the Iranian and Nicaraguan crises in 1978-79.

Lessons drawn from that double debacle — notably by Jeanne Kirkpatrick in "Dictatorships and Double Standards" — virtually determined the initial attitude of the Reagan administration toward the Third World. Later, during the administration's debates over what to do with Ferdinand Marcos of the Philippines, recollections of other, even older Friendly Tyrants episodes influenced thinking. According to observers present, two spectres were loose in the room: Diem and the shah. Diem represented the dangers of doing too much, the shah the dangers of doing too little.

In a way, the presence of both these spectres may have delivered a useful and nuanced warning to those assembled, because U.S. policy in the Philippines was a spactacular success. But, unfortunately, sometimes nothing fails like success; lessons learned incorrectly can be worse than lessons not learned at all. Specifically, the easing out of Ferdinand Marcos and Jean-Claude Duvalier in January-February 1986 led some Reagan administration figures to underestimate the staying power of General Manuel Noriega in Panama. As Elliott Abrams, at that time the assistant secretary of state for Latin America, admitted: "Our experience with Marcos and Duvalier had led us to believe that [economic sanctions] would work. . . . We now realize that it is easier to remove civilian dictators than military ones. In analogous circumstances Marcos and Duvalier were already gone."[5]

Abrams was wrong twice: the Philippine case was not remotely analogous to the one in Panama and, in fact, the United States never imposed economic sanctions against the Marcos government. Success in Haiti, too, had nothing to do with the fact that Jean-Claude Duvalier was only a civilian dictator, and everything to do with the fact that he had no appetite for power while Noriega did.

There are, unfortunately, many ways to fail in dealing with Friendly Tyrants. One can act too soon or too late, use too much force or too little rely too much on allies and multinational organizations or not enough. However one fails, the recriminations at home are often so immense that no Friendly Tyrants failure can be modest — strategically crucial Iran or strategically marginal Nicaragua, it doesn't matter, for these are the mistakes that shake administrations, polemicize debate, and foul the trust between the government and the American people. As the Arab proverb has it: Everything starts small except calamity.

Glasnost and Friendly Tyrants

From the Berlin Blockade in 1948 until very recently, the great majority of Americans agreed that totalitarian communism and Soviet expansionism posed a clear and present danger to the United States. This consensus established the context for the Friendly Tyrants dilemma. In contrast to their long isolationist tradition of staying away from troubles abroad, after 1945 Americans saw internationalism as a lesser evil in the struggle to contain Soviet communism. The United States, which had before linked balance-of-power thinking to the corrupt, decrepit old world, now reluctantly employed balance-of-power strategies itself.

But pursuing such a strategy never came easy, for many if not most Americans remained isolationist at heart. For them, the moral costs of global engagement seemed to outweigh the benefits. From 1945 on, many Americans sought a way back to a simpler role in international life. In this spirit, important voices proclaimed the end of the cold war (and the responsibilities that went with it) as early as the death of Stalin in 1953 and again in 1955, 1963, 1972, and so on until the collapse of the Berlin Wall in 1989.

The Vietnam trauma, in particular, undermined the American postwar consensus; but the Soviet military build-up and geopolitical offensive of the 1970s caused the fundamentals of containment to remain in place through the 1980s. As the decade of the 1990s began, the Soviet-American relationship took on a new cast. With the waning of cold war rhetoric and, in the minds of most Americans, of the Soviet danger itself, the older moral imperatives and isolationist tendencies of American exceptionalism reasserted themselves. In the process, the raison d'être for the basic structure of postwar U.S. foreign policy was eroded.

And so, with a new vigor, Americans are now questioning the useful-ness, cost, and efficacy of the vast structures put in place to make containment an effective policy. Some argue that American commitments exceeded the economy's carrying capacity, and so are counterproductive;[6] others doubt the utility of NATO,[7] the U.S.-Japanese alliance, and ANZUS (Australia, New Zealand, United States).

If close U.S. relationships with democracies are now subjected to skeptical scrutiny, where does that leave alliances with authoritarian and quasi-authoritarian regimes? Entanglements with Friendly Tyrants have been justified for more than forty years as a necessary lesser evil and, clearly, this justification loses force if the greater evil is itself diminishing. If unfriendly tyrants great and small are fading, who needs friendly ones?

This question both eases and complicates the Friendly Tyrants problem. The decline of Soviet bellicosity and the near-absence of prominent Marxist-Leninist insurgencies in the lands of most Friendly Tyrants (exceptions include the Philippines and El Salvador) has changed the world's political climate for the better. But the ever-present discomfort over relations with Friendly Tyrants and the urge to dissociate from them become ever more powerful as the utility of these states in fending off unfriendly tyrants grows less visible. Changes in the world enable the United States to loosen problematical relationships with Friendly Tyrants, and to more vigorously promote human rights and political decency. But slow and careful are the watchwords to bear in mind — history hasn't ended and isn't about to.

Despite all the changes taking place around us, the containment of Soviet power remains an underlying premise of U.S. global commitments, at least for the time being. Soviet policy in the Third World is changing, not ending. There are still places around the world — Afghanistan is one example and Southeast Asia another — where Washington needs to challenge the Soviet leadership to translate fine words into benign practice. Americans should also bear in mind that it was their own sacrifices and activism in the 1980s that helped give rise to Soviet "new thinking" in foreign policy. U.S. bonds with Friendly Tyrants helped this effort in the past and need still to remain a part of it for the foreseeable future, particularly in light of the great uncertainty about the future of Soviet power and policy.

Further, many U.S. interests would require good relations with Friendly Tyrants even if the U.S. and Soviet governments were to become the closest of allies. Even if the cold war is over, a plentitude of other challenges lie ahead, as the Kuwait crisis demonstrated beyond the shadow of a doubt. The U.S. government retains global geopolitical interests, including a need to work with Friendly Tyrants. A number of authoritarian regimes are critical for curtailing drug flows, insuring access to raw materials, opening new markets, stopping terrorism, encouraging regional peacemaking, cooperating on global environmental and health problems, and many other issues. Additionally, it is hard to see how a transformation of Friendly Tyrants into friendly democracies will be aided by U.S. disengagement from them.

It will not be easy for Washington to maintain an activist foreign policy as the black and the white of the cold war fuse into shades of gray. But it must try, for the environment of American foreign policy is growing more complex even as the threat of superpower war recedes. As a consequence, U.S. relations with Friendly Tyrants will surely change. But they will not disappear.

How are we likely to make out? If the past is any guide, the prospects are good. The United States has made many mistakes, with Friendly Tyrants and others, in the last forty-five years. But on the whole, U.S. foreign policy has been reasonably effective in achieving a proper balance of realism and idealism, and that balance has stood us in good stead most of the time.

One thing that can be learned from the Friendly Tyrants experience is that foreign policy problems are rarely solved, but are rather managed. In the future as in the past, realism and idealism will remain inextricably linked in U.S. foreign policy, and that is all to the good. The trick is to maintain the balance on a case-by-case basis, avoiding the extremes of relying on authoritarian regimes in total disregard for our democratic values, or undertaking ideological crusades to spread democracy to peoples and places that are not ready for it and do not wish it.

In the days ahead, American leadership will depend ever more on the skill with which we orchestrate our assets, encompassing both idealism and realism in prudent measure. If policy makers remain alert and sensitive to the maxims presented here, that will be a marginally easier skill to acquire.

Notes

1 See, for example, Patrick Buchanan, "Dusting Off 'Messianic Globaloney,'" *The Washington Times*, September 18, 1989.
2 Two examples include Sandy Vogelgesang, *American Dream, Global Nightmare: The Dilemma of U.S. Human Rights Policy* (New York: W.W. Norton, 1977), and Jonathan Kwitny, *Endless Enemies: The Making of an Unfriendly World* (New York: Congdon and Weed, 1984).
3 Other states tied to a particular system include the two Chinas, Koreas, and (so long as they existed) the two Germanies and Vietnams.
4 Tom Wicker, "'Covert' Means Fiasco," *The New York Times*, October 10, 1989.
5 *The New York Times*, March 28, 1988.

6 Notably, Paul Kennedy, *The Rise and Fall of the Great Powers* (New York: Random House, 1987). Also see Alan Tonelson, "The End of Internationalism?" *The New Republic*, February 13, 1989.

7 Well before the changes of 1989, Melvyn Krauss wrote *How NATO Weakens the West* (New York: Simon and Schuster, 1986), a book whose title explains its thesis.

1: **Beware Dependence**

2: **Be Nimble**

3: **Promote Democracy**

4: **Chastise with Care**

5: **Define Goals**

6: **Know the Country**

7: **Think It Through**

8: **Coordinate Policy**

9: **Hedge Bets**

10: **Plan for Crises**

1 ▪ Beware Dependence

Limit the extent to which U.S. interests depend on Friendly Tyrants. Within such limits, however, pursue beneficial relationships with Friendly Tyrants.

Remember: the greater the American dependence on a Friendly Tyrant, the greater the risk to U.S. interests over time.

Authoritarian regimes promote short term and nonvital American interests much better than long term and vital ones. Persuading a Friendly Tyrant to vote with the United States at the United Nations is one thing, locating major bases on its territory is quite another.

U.S. alliances with democratic countries are blue chip investments; NATO has been the best example, and still is. Alliances with Friendly Tyrants are more in the nature of junk bonds. The smart investor puts most of his money in the former, expecting steady dividends but not spectacular growth. He puts smaller amounts in the latter, which can do very well but which can also go bankrupt. There should be a proportionality between the interests vouchsafed in a government on the one hand and the risks to their safety on the other. When there is no attractive choice, this means at the very least being aware of the risks involved.

The basic point is clear: the United States cannot go it alone all the time, and so choices have to be made between the importance of an interest and the risks of formulating policy within the nexus of a Friendly Tyrants relationship. Prudence suggests that the more important an interest, the more the United States ought to try to go it alone, even at higher cost. And when this is simply not possible, at the very least we ought to keep our eyes wide open about the dangers ahead.

For example, using Mobutu Sese Seko of Zaire to supply Jonas Savimbi's UNITA (União Nacional para a Independência Total de Angola) in the war against the Angolan regime made good sense. It helped to facilitate a partial settlement of southern Africa's problems at relatively low cost. The stake was modest, so was the risk, and it would have made sense even had it not succeeded as it did.

Making Iran a pillar of U.S. foreign policy after 1969 was a very high risk strategy, one that in retrospect appears to have been too high. While Tehran had long been a close ally of the United States, the intensity of the relationship after 1969 boosted the U.S.-Iranian connection to new levels. One can debate whether or not there was much choice in the matter, but the damage done to U.S. interests when the Iranian monarchy fell in 1979 was enormous. On balance, the benefits derived from relations with the shah — a quarter century's alliance with a key country in a crucial region — may have outweighed the price subsequently paid; still, the equation of risks and benefits was skewed after 1969, and the result was a more terrible blow than need have been.

Similar dilemmas exist in other parts of the Middle East, including Saudi Arabia, Jordan, Egypt, and Morocco. Saudi oil and investments remain crucial to Western economies. Jordan is still generally expected to forward the Arab-Israeli peace process, or at least not to obstruct it. Egypt participates in the strategic triangle (along with the United States and Israel) that preserves the bedrock of peace in the region. Moroccan facilities help bind U.S. power between the continental United States and the Levant. None of these governments are as stable as these interests are significant; the price paid for reliance may one day be considerable. But what choice is there?

Staying in the same region, the U.S. government on occasion has found itself inadvertently dependent on a Friendly Tyrant. In the October 1973 Middle East war, the democracies of West Europe turned out to be unreliable while the Caetano regime in Portugal came through, allowing U.S. planes to land at NATO bases in the Azores. As a member of NATO, Portugal was not a typical Friendly Tyrant; still, the next year, Caetano's authoritarian government fell and Portugal nearly became a People's Republic. The Portuguese case demonstrates why relations with Friendly

Tyrants should be pursued (even democratic friends do not always prove constant) at the same time that it points to the risks of relying on them, for had the Portuguese revolution taken place two years earlier, American planes would not have been able to use the Azores in October 1973.

The best way to get things done is to do them yourself, even if it's more expensive that way.

Sometimes the use of allies and proxies makes good sense, but not when the risk exceeds potential benefits. One way to reduce excessive dependence on Friendly Tyrants is simply to take steps to reduce the dependence. These will usually be more cumbersome or expensive, of course, but if the interest warrants it, the switch may be justified. The presence of American soldiers in South Korea limits the extent to which the leaders in Seoul control a vital U.S. interest. Instead of having depended so heavily on Iran for listening stations pointed at the Soviet Union, the U.S. government could have achieved similar capabilities (admittedly at a much higher cost) from space-based assets; when U.S. facilities were lost in 1978, U.S. strategic intelligence was partially blinded for nearly two years.

As for Saudi Arabia in the aftermath of the Gulf war, the United States will maintain bases, pre-position equipment, and enlarge its offshore naval presence. It will also sell arms to Arab friends, not just Saudi Arabia. The point of doing all these things is to maximize within reason local abilities for deterrence and self-defense, so that we will not have to see to them directly, with all the attendant costs. But Saudi Arabia will still not be able to defend itself against a rearmed Iraq, or against Iran. There's nothing wrong with trying to devolve responsibility to local friends — as long as no illusions attend the process.

Unfortunately, sometimes the option of indirect responsibility is either unsatisfactory or unavailable. Naval bases around the globe can in theory be replaced by more aircraft carriers, but the cost would go way up even as capabilities would go way down. Some have argued that dependence on Pakistan for arming the *mujahidin* fighting in Afghanistan could have been reduced by dropping the pretense of a covert operation. This is not so; Pakistan would have prohibited transit and made the operation impossible. There was no choice.

Again, being self-reliant does not mean that there is no role in U.S. policy for U.S. allies or multilateral organizations. Such roles exist and they are important; those reserved for Friendly Tyrants, however, should be limited and scrutinized hard.

Don't send either too large or too small an arsenal to a Friendly Tyrant; help it to defend its territory but not to commit aggression against foreign enemies.

Politics sometimes has a way of getting ahead of military inventories or supply relationships. U.S. weapons were delivered to Greece before the April 1967 coup for one purpose but the junta used them for another. This was bad luck, not bad judgment, but bad judgment happens, too. Weapons sold to Iran after 1969 caused two problems. Firstly, the shah fielded an army in Oman during the mid-1970s, raising the prospect of direct conflict between Iran and South Yemen, which could have had wide consequences. Secondly, the huge arsenal sent to the shah for the sake of insuring regional security was used by Khomeini for exactly the opposite purpose. Of course, other states would have sold weapons to a cash-rich Iran, but other countries could not have provided the huge and sophisticated arsenal that the United States did.

There was a possibility in 1977 that Sadat would use U.S. weapons to invade Libya, but he dared not do so without American permission — which the Carter administration refused to grant. On balance, the U.S. government has rarely let the tail of its military supply relationship with Friendly Tyrants wag the dog of U.S. policy, for states are usually unwilling to jeopardize the supply relationship with unauthorized uses.

Finally, it is possible to send too few weapons, as well. Congress was unwise to deny aid and weapons to the South Vietnamese government in 1974-75, because what replaced it has been much worse for American interests, regional interest, and the interests of the Vietnamese people.

A less dramatic example concerns Tunisia. The regime of Habib Bourguiba was a staunch friend of the United States, but the United States government provided too little aid to hold Libya's Colonel Qadhdhafi at bay — hence the disturbing Gafsa incident of 1980, in which the Libyan government was complicit in aggression against Tunisian territory.

Do everything possible to make sure that American aid is not used for domestic repression.

It is reasonable for Washington to help Friendly Tyrants confront communist or otherwise aggressive insurgencies; but great care must be taken to insure that the regime does not use the American aid to bolster its domestic position by increasing repression. No matter what the U.S. government does, however, it cannot always have absolute confidence that U.S. military aid will not be misused.

In a few cases, this malign linkage has actually existed, as in South Vietnam in the 1960s and in Somoza's Nicaragua before 1978. More often, domestic critics of the U.S. government seize on dubious evidence to make this point. Such was the case in South Korean and the Philippines. The supposed government-linked "death squads" of El Salvador may well fit the same pattern, although the Salvadoran case is rather complicated. Some observers go so far as to accuse Washington of aiding repression in countries that are not especially friendly, like Burma.[1]

It is not always easy, of course, to distinguish between legitimate security needs and repression. The U.S. government trained the Panamanian defense forces when General Noriega was a Friendly Tyrant. When he became an unfriendly tyrant, not only did he use this force to intimidate Panamanians and bloody the May 1989 election, but the U.S. government was forced to confront elements of it when it went into Panama in December 1989.

In El Salvador, as noted above, the problem has been different and more complex. The Duarte regime reduced the autonomy of the Salvadoran military to some degree, but it has increased again in the difficult period of the Cristiani government. The military, in turn, may or may not have control over so-called "death squads" but that is almost beside the point. The point is that the U.S. government has not been able to deal with the civilian authorities in the country with any reasonable expectation that they can control the use of American weapons that are delivered. But if the weapons had not been delivered, the FMLN (Farabundo Martí de Liberación Nacional) might have won the war. As things appear to have turned out, a strong Salvadoran military response has convinced the FMLN to negotiate an end to the war, as their participation in February 1991 elections seems to attest.

What to do in the tough cases like El Salvador? There are no catch-all rules here. All anyone can do is assess what is at stake on a case-by-case basis, and decide whether it is worth taking a chance to provide aid.

Avoid the "sunken costs" trap.

Changing the course of U.S. policy is sometimes deterred by a sensitivity to obligations and investments already incurred. This can lead to throwing good money after bad — always a bad idea. Many examples can be found, some major, some not.

A mild example concerns U.S. policy toward Samuel Doe's Liberia. Before Sgt. Doe came to power in 1980, Liberia had been developed into a significant strategic asset. Listening posts, naval facilities, and economic interests were already firm. Mr. Doe's coup was violent, his rule was brutal, his regime widely hated. But the United States government provided more than $500 million worth of aid between 1980 and 1985 anyway, fearing to jeopardize already sunken costs, even though it *knew* that Doe's tenure was unpopular, fragile, and unlikely to last very long. In the end, however, Washington avoided getting sucked in too deeply. In his crisis in the summer and autumn of 1990, Doe called on the United States, in the person of the President Bush, to help him. Wisely, President Bush demurred.

A similar if sadder story concerns the Greek coup of April 1967. Costs sunken in Greece, and associated with NATO, were much larger and had deeper roots. U.S. reluctance to react strongly to the coup, either at the time, or later, was affected by sunken costs. In the end, the failure to react, and the provision of more aid, did not protect American interests very well when the junta fell in 1974.

A current case involves El Salvador. Now that the Sandinistas are out of power in Managua, and the Salvadoran government and rebels seem embarked on a course of political settlement, no compelling reason exists for the levels of U.S. aid and attention still lavished on that unfortunate little country. Sunken costs are the only reason the United States remains involved.

Most striking of all when it comes to sunken costs is the example of South Vietnam. By the time it became clear in Washington that South Vietnam was in imminent danger of falling to the communists in the 1963-64 period, sunken costs in Indochina (which went back to the support of the French war effort between 1949 and 1954) seemed enormous. Prestige, advisors, and high velocity careers represent other forms of sunken costs as well. In the case of Vietnam, the U.S. government simply could not drag itself back despite the general awareness within the bureaucracy that the United States was not winning the war and had no prospect of winning it in the near term. The actuarial mentality of the "whiz kids" in Robert S. McNamara's Pentagon, if anything, emphasized still further the obsession with relative costs and (elusive) benefits.

Since interests often change faster than policy, review bilateral relations at the expert level on a regular basis.

Once installed, a policy develops an institutional life of its own. Established relations tend to be retained out of inertia and force of habit. Routine can be helpful for it allows top policy makers to concentrate on the crises of the moment. But routine can be harmful, too. Unless something dramatic happens, decisions beget themselves. The problem is that the "something" that happens is rarely pleasant, especially when it comes to Friendly Tyrants.

Examples of this problem are plentiful. In some cases, American involvement should decrease. Even though UNITA's value in helping get the Cubans out of Angola essentially ended in early 1989, American aid to UNITA continued unabated. Aid to Zaire continued at high levels for a time, too, even though the regional environment had much improved.

In other cases, a regime gains in importance, need, or capability. The number of American troops in South Korea remains unchanged even though the capability of South Korean forces has improved dramatically, while tensions on the peninsula have diminished. In the late 1970s and early 1980s, Turkey's importance to the United States grew, owing to events in Iran and Afghanistan, at a time when Turkish democracy was strained by subversion and economic difficulty. But Congress insisted on maintaining a seven-to-ten ratio of aid to Greece and Turkey. This effectively limited U.S. aid to Turkey and, partly as a result, the Turkish military briefly intervened to restore order.

To institutionalize vigilance in government is difficult but not impossible. Interagency groups can make use of B-Team, or "devil's advocate," outsiders who comment on staff work. National Intelligence Estimates (NIEs) have proven to be, on their own, inadequate tools of review, but the value of NIEs lies mostly in their writing as opposed to what they actually say. The process itself forces assumptions and expectations to come out in the open. This is not the same as solving a problem, but it does make analysts more aware of changes in bilateral relations. Should crisis strike, key issues will at least have been discussed; this may be called the "I know it when I see it" phenomenon.

Just as the furnace in the basement requires regular, periodic maintenance, so do ties to Friendly Tyrants. Neglect either a machine or a relationship for long enough, and you are asking for trouble.

Note

1 See Andrew Sullivan, "Burma Breaks," *The New Republic*, September 5, 1988.

2 Be Nimble

Fundamental U.S. interests are usually tied to good relations with a country, not with a particular individual or regime; therefore, avoid gratuitous gestures of friendship toward today's rulers, and you will have less gratuitous trouble with tomorrow's.

Don't let relations with a dictator wax any warmer than needed.
There is a world of difference between maintaining proper relations with a Friendly Tyrant and gushing forth with praise about him. That's what LaGuardia was trying to point out in the epigram above: symbolic flourishes may look good, but you can't eat them — they are no substitute for securing concretely one's interests.

Jean Giradoux put it even more graphically; he once remarked that it is the privilege of the great to witness catastrophe from a balcony. How true! Nelson Rockefeller, serving as a presidential emissary to Haiti, publicly wrapped his arms around young Jean-Claude Duvalier on a balcony in Port-au-Price in 1969. Jimmy Carter threw his arms around the shah of Iran on another balcony in Tehran on New Year's Eve 1978, toasting his rule for creating an island of stability in a turbulent region.

Commerce Secretary Maurice Stans, Vice-President Spiro Agnew, and Secretary of Defense Melvin Laird all visited Greece in 1969-1970; the junta played up these visits for all they were worth, which was quite a lot. General Galtieri of Argentina drank too much liquor and received too many compliments on his visit to Washington in 1981; this encouraged him and his colleagues to imagine that their attempt to seize the Falkland Islands would meet with U.S. neutrality or even support.

Also, democratic oppositions sometimes reason from such public displays of affection that the U.S. government would never allow their success, even though at times Washington might have welcomed it. Dictators know this and so use their cordial ties with American presidents to dissuade democratic opposition forces from even trying to challenge their rule.

Vice-President George Bush, in Manila after the Philippine elections of 1981, praised Ferdinard Marcos's "devotion to democracy." This remark was not only untrue and unnecessary, but counterproductive in precisely this way. Few dictators have ever showed more skill than Marcos at exploiting his American connections to intimidate his adversaries. This was true not only at the 1981 inauguration, but during Marcos's state visit to Washington in 1982 and on several other occasions subsequently.

In particular, some Friendly Tyrants try to exploit the U.S. media to show how important and respected they are. Ferdinand Marcos frequently ordered Philippine television to show him as he appeared on American television, the implicit message being that Marcos was so major an international figure and so esteemed by the American leaders, opposition forces should not even bother to try to unseat him. Mobutu Sese Seko in Zaire occasionally resorted to this tactic; every public act of his in the United States is taped for use back home. American journalists and politicians are usually oblivious to this use of their prestige. They would do well to pay more attention. Just who is using whom, who is observing and who is being observed, is not always clear.

Even throwaway gestures are significant, for the United States often looms larger abroad than Americans realize. The actions of its leaders may carry far more weight in a place like Iran than in the United States itself. Minor votes in a Senate sub-committee or statements by the state department spokesman routinely show up as headlines in distant countries. A competent foreign policy requires close attention to image as well as substance. Protocol with Friendly Tyrants demands serious attention.

Richard Nixon may not have followed his own advice, but what he said is nevertheless true: reserve a "warm embrace" for allied democracies and offer only a "firm handshake" to Friendly Tyrants.[1]

Do not suffocate a Friendly Tyrant with too many visible American connections.

Too many American connections can undermine a dictator's nationalist credentials and make him appear to be an agent of the U.S. government. This is the foreign policy version of the kiss of death. To know how and when to be inconspicuous is sublime strategic wisdom.

South Vietnam started its brief life in 1954 as an independent non-communist country. But then, in an effort to win the war against Hanoi, the Americans shouldered aside their Vietnamese allies. The war's administration was Americanized in 1963, the fighting was American-ized two years later. The size of the American presence made it overbearing and prevented the South Vietnamese government from developing its own legitimacy. Treating the Vietnamese virtually like children (cute but incompetent), designing military strategy (search and destroy missions) without consideration for political factors, and tempting them to corruption beyond their wildest dreams, the U.S. government sapped Saigon's moral strength, reduced its capacities, and uprooted its citizenry.

In Iran, too, there were altogether too many Americans — business-men, soldiers, teachers, advisors of various sorts — after 1969. Their presence had the unintended effect of eroding the shah's credentials as a nationalist. In fact, his behavior at the time should have gained him credit on these grounds, for he used Iran's oil wealth to distance himself from the United States and after the first oil shock of 1973-74, the shah actually had the upper hand in the U.S.-Iranian relationship. But try as he may, the shah could never shake the conviction of many Iranians that he was a U.S. puppet.

Skeptics have pointed out that before 1975 the largest U.S. embassy in the world was in South Vietnam. When Saigon fell, the embassy in Iran inherited the mantle. When the shah fell, the embassy in Egypt took first honors — a sign of trouble ahead? Certainly, the fear of leaving too many Americans in the Arabian peninsula after the war for Kuwait is very well-based, indeed.

The risk of overexposure today is probably most acute in Egypt and South Korea. Both are critical to U.S. interests, so there is not much room to pull back the commitment.

The Korean case may be the most delicate because of the fundamental changes taking place in that country. The country has grown up and it is only natural that this include an expanded sense of national mission, one that disparages old conditions. The presence of Americans in too-powerful posts for too long seems to be taking its toll in South Korea. The United States is part of the old conditions, and the presence of its troops, especially if out in the open, is like a thorn in this new sense of pride.

Other countries, potentially no less important, pose fewer dilemmas these days. Americans are not overexposed in Indonesia, Kenya, or Zaire. They should stay that way.

With Friendly Tyrants, less is more. But in some cases it is not the absolute size of the U.S. presence that irritates but its high public profile. The sensitivity of the Spanish government to the U.S. air force base in Torrejón had similar roots. Torrejón was so close to Madrid that the comings and goings of U.S. planes were constantly noticed in the capital, and served as a constant reminder of the origins of the U.S. alliance in the Franco period. This affronted the democratic Spanish government, and the base was closed. Had the Nixon administration chosen to close Torrejón in the 1969-1970 base negotiations, and used its less visible (and underutilized) bases at Zaragoza and Morón de la Frontera, things might have turned out much differently. In this connection, it is worth noting that American bases in the Azores are so far from Lisbon that they remind no one of Salazar, bother few Portuguese, and raise few political hackles.

Criticism can sometimes negate the kiss-of-death syndrome. American criticism of President Zia ul-Haq in Pakistan, mainly from the Congress, helped Zia demonstrate proper distance from the United States to his key domestic constituencies. The White House wanted Zia to stay in power for the sake of arming the Afghan rebels, so Congressional criticism actually played into the administration's hands.

Aging Friendly Tyrants are the most dangerous, so American diplomats should watch them closely and keep their overnight bags packed.

As the years go by, most Friendly Tyrants aspire to monopolize power and public life. Left to its own devices, authoritarianism tends toward totalitarianism in governments just as egoism tends toward megalomania in individuals. This is the Caligula syndrome and historians know it well.

Trujillo and Batista became more brutal, more demanding, more intrusive of other domains of society as their tenures lengthened. So did Rhee, the shah, Marcos, and Noriega. So has Siad Barre in Somalia. Even now, President Suharto in Indonesia is trying to make himself independent of his power base in the army to become the dominant political institution in the country. The Caligula syndrome often spells the beginning of the end for tyrants. It represents an overstretching of their capabilities and a violation of local political norms.

Should the U.S. government wish to preserve a Friendly Tyrant, the tyrant must not be easily allowed to use the American connection to contribute to this process. If the United States government wishes to discuss a renewal of basing rights in a given country, for example, it should try to deal with the appropriate government ministries whenever possible, and not allow a megalomaniacal tyrant to monopolize and claim credit for the agreement. U.S. aid must be carefully monitored to insure that it does not go to building imperial palaces and monuments. Admittedly, this is very hard to do, but the effort must still be made.

Most important of all, the tyrant must not be allowed to muzzle tactful U.S. criticism of human rights abuses, or he may conclude that he can do anything whatsoever. Indeed, if that becomes the case, he might be right.

Associate the American government with evolving democratic processes, not with individuals or parties.

Rather than depend on particular individuals, political organizations, or ideological currents, the U.S. government should stress processes and institutions — a free press, unfettered labor organizing, fair elections, civic education. Our business is democracy and our interests depend on its health, not on persons and their particular institutional props. We pride ourselves on being a government of laws, not men; we should recognize the same principle in our foreign policy.

Failure to understand this precept can be downright counterproductive to the evolution and solidification of a democratic political culture. U.S. involvement in Greek politics in the late 1940s and 1950s, and in Chilean politics in the 1950s and 1960s, are cases in point; in both instances, Washington backed pro-U.S. elements (what came to form the National Radical Union in Greece and the Christian Democrats in Chile) without understanding fully how that support undermined their nationalist credentials, or how other anticommunist forces interpreted U.S. support. The lapse of democracy in both cases owed at least something to an anti-Americanism that developed out of perceptions of U.S. political favoritism.

The recruitment of the South Korean elite after World War II is open to similar criticism, as was the reconstituting of the Philippine government after the return of American forces in 1945-46. The American attempt to reinstall the pre-war elites, even including politicians who had cooperated publicly with the Japanese occupiers, planted the seeds for the anti-U.S. opposition that even today threatens the Aquino government.

Finally in this regard, the Bush administration has had to walk a fine line between insisting that the al-Sabah dynasty be reinstated in Kuwait and accepting the nondemocratic character of that government. Certainly, when the reinstated al-Sabah's appeared initially to be denying the aspirations of Kuwaitis, and even gunning for opposition figures according to some reports, it put the United States in a difficult spot. When Kuwaitis were reported to be using Iraqi methods (and even devices) of torture on

Palestinians and others believed complicit with Iraqi aggression, it raised still more problems, as well it should.

Don't assume that allies must share U.S. ideological precepts to be useful.

It was never necessary that allied governments think just like Washington about communism. Allies need to share enough values to be useful, but not so many that they look like lackeys. In the late 1940s and 1950s, many American policy makers had a difficult time understanding that democratic socialists in some countries could be more credible and effective opponents of local communists and pro-Soviet elements than conservatives. An argument can be made, again from the Greek example, that singleminded U.S. support for Greek conservatives pushed middle-of-the-road socialists into the cynical arms of the Greek far Left.

Along parallel lines, when the U.S. government does not support conservative forces too closely or openly, as in Portugal in 1975, its restraint can take the wind out of the anti-American forces. In El Salvador, support for the Christian Democrats under Duarte weakened the FMLN but, ironically, excessive U.S. identification with Duarte may have produced a voter backlash that brought the right-wing government of Alfredo Cristiani into power.

In South Africa, support for moderate forces — white and black alike — aims to make it harder for the African National Congress (ANC) to insinuate a link between the U.S. government and Afrikaner extremists; or for such extremists to insinuate a link between the U.S. government and the ANC. In Chile, supporting democracy, not Pinochet, before the October 1988 plebiscite, and evident neutrality in the November 1989 election, stripped the Chilean far Left of its anti-American weapon against the candidate of the Center and moderate Left, Patricio Aylwin.

Building democracy depends on creating new attitudes, institutions, and expectations about public life. If the U.S. government ties itself not to these but to specific individuals and parties, it risks undermining the evolution of democracy. While some political interventions may have been on balance worthwhile, tying the prestige of the U.S. government to rulers and parties carries a heavy price, for American favoritism is long remembered and resented.

Stay in touch with all political factions in a country, even if a Friendly Tyrant objects.

The U.S. government has repeatedly been caught out of touch, ignorant of the forces threatening a client regime. Some of the time, this was due to its own nearsightedness and neglect, not a ruler's strictures. Many policy makers in Washington in the Carter administration never understood how deeply Marxist the Sandinista opposition was, even though the Sandinistas made no secret of their views. American intelligence in Portugal in 1974 was also poor; Washington's information base in that crisis was so narrow that the policy's success was all the more notable.

At other times, however, U.S. myopia was indeed a function of undue sensitivity to a dictator's wishes. Always looking over his shoulder, the Friendly Tyrant is naturally uneasy when American diplomats invite his adversaries to dinner. Clearly, there is no reason to upset a useful Friendly Tyrant gratuitously. But maintaining contact with opposition forces is far from gratuitous.

For thirty-five years, a succession of American presidents embraced Shah Mohammed Reza Pahlavi of Iran. Religious opposition to the shah was ignored in Washington, in large part because Washington assumed that opposition would come from the Left, from the Tudeh Party and its associates. To appease the shah, the Americans accepted that the Central Intelligence Agency (CIA) depend for information on SAVAK, its Iranian counterpart. Along with the shah, then, the U.S. government lost touch with what was going on in the streets. A vicious circle developed: the less U.S. diplomats and intelligence officials knew, the more they depended on official Iranian informants. When the revolution came, Americans knew next to nothing about the mullahs who took power, and had almost no contacts with them.

Sometimes, admittedly, there are few choices. When the Greek colonels overthrew democracy in April 1967, the U.S. government found itself with extensive investments in a country that was suddenly a Friendly Tyrant. There were no democratic processes to support; the coup was ruthless and thorough. Withdrawing the U.S. investment was not prudent or perhaps even possible; so Washington should have done more to restore democracy by pressuring the colonels. One way would have been to enlarge liaison with Greek opposition politicians in exile, and let the junta know it. But this was not done.

Staying in touch does not mean, however, public meetings at high levels. Secretary of State George P. Shultz's decision to welcome Oliver Tambo, the head of the African National Congress, to his office in 1988 was quite a risk. This meeting went beyond information gathering and served to bestow legitimacy on an organization that did not deserve it at that time. Although in retrospect, changes in South Africa make Shultz's gesture appear farsighted, that still does not make it wise. As the witch in *The Wizard of Oz* put it, "These things must be done delicately."

Don't assume that American support for an authoritarian regime necessarily makes its opponents anti-American.

It is wrong to assume the U.S. government is always going to reap the whirlwind when a Friendly Tyrant falls. Ideology and political culture are more important than the mere fact that the U.S. government supported a now-deposed tyrant. The Iranian case is most apposite. During the political crisis of the shah, and even into the early stages of the revolution before Khomeini consolidated power, practically every group in Iranian politics outside of the fundamentalists hoped for American support.

Another example: Despite ten years of support for Samuel Doe in Liberia, the rebel forces led by Charles Taylor and Prince Johnson were far from anti-American — indeed, they were quite the reverse. A little coolness toward a faltering Mr. Doe at the end, in August and September 1990, was all it took to wash away most of the remembrance of the previous decade of U.S. support.

In other cases, U.S. support for the old regime does prejudice new rulers against the United States, but such prejudice need not be decisive, long lasting, or unmovable. Greece under the colonels offers an example. Support from Washington for the colonels made much of the Greek opposition anti-American, but not all of it. Constantine Karamanlis, the centrist politician who eventually picked up the pieces when the colonels fell in 1974, remained positively disposed to the United States. He waited in Paris for the telephone to ring from Washington with support for his new government when he found himself on the verge of coming to power. Nothing happened. Ultimately, Karamanlis could not put off the challenge of the leftist Pan-Hellenic Socialist Movement (PASOK) under Andreas Papandreou, and U.S.-Greek relations entered free fall. Arguably, had the U.S. government been more helpful to centrist Greek democrats during and just after the fall of the junta, PASOK might have never come to power.

Contrarily, oppositions in power cannot always be bought off; Marxist-Leninists are almost always of this ilk, but few others are. Thus, the Carter administration was wrong to believe that it could "learn to live" with the Sandinista victory in Nicaragua. This erroneous belief inspired Washington to become a major donor of economic aid to the new regime in 1979-1980 — money which was used to fuel the insurgency in El Salvador. For their part, the Sandinistas hinted that no dose of reparations from Washington would ever be large enough to set the historical ledger straight, in effect leaving U.S. policy makers in a policy vacuum of their own making.

Don't give up the ship — it's never too late to get on the winning side of a Friendly Tyrants crisis.

Breaking with a tyrant and gaining favor with the elements coming to power is sometimes less difficult to do than might be expected.

Even after fourteen years of tolerating Marcos's martial law regime, the U.S. government made a dramatic reversal in the Philippines in 1985-86, with major implications for relations with the new leaders. Long years of cool-hearted support — but support all the same — for Baby Doc Duvalier notwithstanding, Washington also got credit for ousting him among many Haitians — even though it abandoned him only at the last minute.

The Reagan administration's policy toward Chile, switching from support for Pinochet to benign neutrality to support for the opposition, changed just in time to land on the winning side of the October 1988 plebiscite. U.S. forces were cheered and welcomed after overthrowing Noriega in Panama in December 1989, even though most Panamanians thought of Noriega as having been a product of U.S. policy, and despite the generalized pain inflicted on Panama by U.S. sanctions.

All of this only goes to show either that people have poor memories, or that when all is said and done, gratitude based on concrete interests is more important than grudges in most of those circumstances when new regimes need help.

Note

1   Richard Nixon, *Six Crises* (New York: Doubleday, 1962), pp. 191-92.

3 Promote Democracy

An ounce of prevention is worth a pound of cure.
— Benjamin Franklin

You can fool some of the people all of the time and all of the people some of the time — and that should be sufficient for most purposes.
— not Abraham Lincoln

U.S. foreign policy should be biased in favor of democratic allies and toward the promotion of democracy in the lands of Friendly Tyrants. This makes sense not just because it is morally right, but because it is pragmatic abroad (ties with democracies are low risk compared to those with Friendly Tyrants) and at home (Americans more readily accept relations with Friendly Tyrants when these are seen as temporary lesser evils about which the U.S. government is not complacent).

Favor democracies over autocracies whenever there is a realistic choice.
This is less banal than it sounds, for it is very tempting to deal with Friendly Tyrants. So long as the tyrant is firmly in charge, deals can be cut quickly and at the top. There is no muss and fuss with foreign domestic opinion or parliaments; there are fewer leaks, and no elections to foil or reverse the deal. Democratic politics, on the other hand, represent the open clash of different points of view in free competition, and therefore are usually less settled. Untidiness is a natural characteristic of democracy, and its enthusiasms often affect foreign policy.

Still, when the choice exists, the U.S. government must not fall prey to the temptation of dealing with pliant dictatorships at the expense of democratic states. It is always in the long-term American interest for allies to shed their Friendly Tyrants status and become democracies.

Turkey and Greece offer relevant examples of the tempestuous nature of democratic politics. The worst periods of Turkish-American relations came at times when democracy was flourishing in Turkey, notably after the 1974 Cyprus crisis. But these problems were weathered; Turkey became a vibrant democracy, and today U.S.-Turkish relations are excellent. Had Turkey remained under military rule, and had the U.S. government encouraged this, relations today would surely be more troubled.

The Greek case is less salutary. Washington's difficulties with the Greek governments from 1974 to 1989 were due in part to the poisonous legacy of U.S. support for the Greek junta between 1967 and 1974 and, long before the advent of the colonels, U.S. support for conservative elements in Greece after 1947, some of whom were seen as (and may well have been) collaborators with the Germans during the Nazi occupation of Greece. Nevertheless, despite the difficulties of these years, most of which were manufactured from the Greek side, the U.S. government wisely turned the other cheek. Implicit in this was the hope that Greece being a democracy, the anti-Americans would disgrace themselves in due course. They did. The fall of the Papandreou government in June 1989 promised improved U.S.-Greek relations and better NATO cooperation.

Encourage democracy in Friendly Tyrants up to, but not beyond, the point of destabilizing an ally for which no better regime replacement exists.

Democracy has many virtues. Although not wholly immune to adopting aggressive policies, democratic governments almost never make war on each other (the only significant exception being the War of 1812, and even that depends on whether one believes that Britain qualifies as having been a democracy then). They pursue more predictable policies. The authorities treat their citizens better. Institutional structures are more open to change. Democratic allies are likely to share a broader range of interests.

Failing full-fledged democracy itself, a healthy process of democratization is the next best condition to have in an American ally. Democratization is functional: reducing the number of tyrannies is the best way to reduce the potential for Friendly Tyrants crises. To the extent that the U.S. government succeeds in helping to build democracies or to restore them, it puts the Friendly Tyrants syndrome behind.

And while building democracy is an exceedingly difficult task, taking democracy as its theme causes American foreign policy to thrive abroad and be popular at home. Indeed, encouraging democracy is one of the few axioms of American foreign policy that attracts wide domestic support in nearly all places and times, for it combines the two usually distinct imperatives of American life, the moral and the national interest. These concerns bring nearly the whole nation together, a crucial matter in a country where public opinion plays such an important role.

Now, consensus is not always possible, nor is it desirable if the consensus is wrongheaded; after all, not all minds that think alike are great. But domestic politics require the president to build up political capital by compromising. If he wants to pursue unpopular policies — such as arming Cambodian rebels associated with the Khmer Rouge before July 1990, or aiding Friendly Tyrants — he must give in on other issues. One obvious place to build such capital to do unpopular but sometimes necessary things is by supporting democracy whenever possible. The October 1988 plebiscite in Chile, for example, created the hope of an era of good feeling in Congress, the press, and the lobbies. Supporting the February 1990 elections in Nicaragua as a democratic opening even required channeling modest amounts of aid to the Sandinistas, an "unfriendly tyrant," but things worked out rather well.

Keeping these considerations in mind, it appears that the Reagan administration did not do enough in 1988 to support, even symbolically, the democratic opposition in Burma. The failure to abridge normal relations with China in any significant way in the wake of the massacre in Tiananmen Square in June 1989 was wrong, too. Totally ignoring democracy in considering the political reconstruction of Iraq in the aftermath of the Persian Gulf war was also peculiar, and did little to help the true friends of democracy in the Arab world, a small but important group that looks to the United States for support.

Ignoring democracy — or merely being perceived to ignore democracy — often carries a high price. Some democrats in Latin America claim to be anti-U.S. because the U.S. government for so long supported Latin military dictatorships. In fact, U.S. policy has been more nuanced than that. The United States has supported some dictatorships, but it has also pressured dictatorships. Besides, suffering a regime is not the same as supporting it, and it is unfair to insist that U.S. policy demand that Latin Americans be more democratic than they themselves have wanted to be.

Nevertheless, these long years of real or apparent cynicism toward Latin America have bequeathed a problem to Washington. Today, supporting oligarchs means aligning with a group repugnant to most Americans and insuring instability in Latin America for as long as the old elite are in power. Sometimes, the oligarchs will lose power to anti-American forces, such as the Sandinistas. But U.S. government support for those urging basic reform and social justice risks bringing anti-U.S. forces into power, too. Washington cannot afford to be blindly and single-mindedly supportive of either the old elite or of the rising opposition, especially since so many dissidents renounce their populist promises when they reach power, and in turn rule undemocratically themselves.

There are other cases, too, where the ruling elite is distinctly more pro-American than the population at large. In such cases, more democracy would probably lead to a less cordial relationship even if it stabilizes the country. Mexico under the PRI may have fit this category ten years ago, although not today. Interestingly, the majority of such cases nowadays come from the Muslim world, including Pakistan under Zia, Iran under the shah, Saudi Arabia under the Saudi dynasty, nearly all the small Persian Gulf states, Jordan under King Hussein, Egypt under Sadat and Mubarak, and Morocco under King Hasan.

Don't use American power against democratically elected or locally legitimate governments.

U.S. intervention to depose an elected government or a government otherwise legitimate in the eyes of most of its people — as with the Arbenz government in Guatemala in 1954 — is never advisable. The long term damage of such efforts outweighs short term relief, both in the country in question and in the United States.

In the country in question, it must be assumed that if a government is elected or is otherwise legitimate by local standards, then lots of people will be angered by foreign intervention, overt or covert, to depose it. For the United States the problem is especially acute, because the United States stands for democracy and self-determination in the world at large. Such interventions paint the United States as hypocritical in the country in question and beyond. Such an image is not just unpleasant but palpably damaging.

Also, recriminations at home from such adventures, with idealists invariably pitted against realists, are inevitable and leave a bitter after-taste. One consequence in the late 1970s was the emasculation of American intelligence institutions. Indeed, so strong is the domestic antipathy to such interventions, some people see them even when they did not occur, as with the U.S. role in Allende's Chile in 1972. While many people believe that the United States tried to overthrow Allende, the truth is murkier. Before the election, the United States tried to help defeat him and failed. After the election but before the inauguration, the CIA tried to prevent him from taking office, but its plan backfired completely. After the inauguration, the United States worked only to preserve the integrity of an independent opposition, not to oust Allende.

Happily, this precept is widely understood and appreciated. Outside of the Arbenz case and the popular but partially mistaken interpretation of U.S. policy toward Chile, it is hard to think of many prominent or recent American transgressions here. Some point to the overthrow of Mohammed Mossadegh in Iran in 1953; but Dr. Mossadegh was never elected to the premiership, had no broad political mandate, controlled no political party, and ruled through emergency decrees at the time of his ousting. Other possible cases include U.S. actions in Brazil (1961-64), Ecuador (1960-63), and Costa Rica (mid-1950s), but the evidence is neither clear nor compelling in most of these cases.[1]

Seek good relations with all democratic countries, even those few whose governments are tempestuous or anti-American ...

Democratic countries do not always get along with each other. Aside from problems with Greece and Turkey at the fullness of their democracies, the United States has had its share of heartaches from democratic governments in Spain, Sweden, France, Israel, and even New Zealand. But the wonderful thing about democracies is that government ultimately reflects the will of the people, and governments change. If the United States sincerely addresses itself to democratic countries, eventually, when the government changes, there will be some chance of an improved relationship. One of the big problems with Friendly Tyrants is that if their friendliness wanes — as with General Noriega — the U.S. government can entertain no expectations of an eventual improvement as long as the dictator remains in power.

In recent years, there has been only one consistently anti-American democracy — India — but there have been lesser examples and there might soon be others. The Sudanese government of Sadiq al-Mahdi was democratically elected, but not friendly toward the United States. Free elections at the municipal level in Algeria in June 1990 pointed the way for an Islamic government to come to power. Such a government would be democratic but probably anti-American. So would a truly democratic government in Jordan.

Washington should try to befriend such regimes anyway, if only to undercut the regime's use of anti-American propaganda themes and to build up a reservoir of good will against the day that the temper of the times should change. If real democracies emerge and maintain themselves, they will probably seek better relations eventually.

. . . But don't let democracy be the only criterion by which policy is decided.

India is not just a huge country that American officials would like to separate from its Soviet sponsor; it is also a democracy. Cool U.S.-Indian relations fly in the face of the theory of democratic comity like no other relationship on earth, and it is natural for the U.S. government to want to rectify the anomaly. But the occasional U.S. effort to befriend India makes sense only as long as it does not come at the expense of the U.S. relationship with Pakistan. That is so when Pakistan is a democracy, as it was briefly under Benazir Bhutto in 1989-1990, and when it is not, as it has been for most of the last forty years. Why?

There are times when the structure of geopolitics points so sharply that little can be done to efface its impact. India is aligned with the Soviet Union because these two states share a major regional rival, China. Insofar as the Sino-Indian relationship is unlikely to improve qualitatively, India will continue to seek close ties with the Soviet Union, irrespective of ideology. Pakistan, more or less by default, seeks good relations with China, and since the United States has been more worried about Moscow than Beijing since the 1970s, that, too, sustains the U.S.-Pakistani relationship. As long as the United States government wishes to maintain a strategic partnership with China to balance Soviet power, Washington is stuck with Islamabad and against New Delhi. If U.S.-Soviet relations change to the point where the United States no longer wishes to keep the so-called China "card," then major changes in U.S. policy in the subcontinent become possible and even likely. But not until. And in all this, in the past as well as the present and future, communism and democracy have precious little to do with it, for better or for worse.

Generously support Friendly Tyrants who evolve into democrats . . .

Not much can be done to push well-established authoritarian rulers toward elections, but something can be done to help protect fledgling democracies against their predators. In trying to protect frail democracies, the U.S. government should keep a few basic rules in mind: help build democratic institutions, speak up for the new government, assist the economy, supply weapons (if needed), and oppose military involvement in politics.[2]

Tyrants often mess up the economy, either by raiding the public purse to enrich themselves and their friends or by following policies designed to keep an elite in power. In Latin America especially, statist economic policy has frequently dovetailed closely with the dictatorial penchant for buying patronage with public funds. Although there are exceptions — Pinochet's Chile was a stunning economic success — it follows generally that the dictators must go if vibrant Latin economies are to develop.

It follows in turn that new democracies need to show more economic competence than the tyrannies. This is not always easy to do. Especially at first, democratic regimes tend to have economic difficulties, in part because they have to clean up their predecessors' profligate legacy by raising taxes or cutting spending. The average citizen may not understand this and conclude that things were better under the army; popular opinion in Argentina and Guatemala in the late 1980s reflects this illusion.

Alternately, economics may serve as the engine of democratic growth. Clearly, East Asian countries under authoritarian rule are pertinent here. Here the tyrants did not destroy the economy, but built it up. They were not usurpers, but autocratic modernizers. In Thailand, South Korea, and Taiwan, economic growth has had profound social implications, softening autocratic rule and promoting political pluralism. In such cases, the U.S. government needs to manage its evolving trading relations in such a way that successful open economies do not get the idea that the U.S. government is punishing them for their success. To be a bully in international trade in order to make up for domestic economic shortcomings — a role that, unfortunately, the U.S. government has sometimes assumed of late — has implications that transcend economics.

... But use American money intelligently or don't use it at all.

Easing the transition from a statist economy to a market economy does not mean funds spread indiscriminately. Foreign aid is often a waste of money, or worse; it distorts the economy of a developing state and makes it less self-sufficient. Intelligently done, however, assistance can make painful economic adjustments politically more palatable. Unlike much so-called foreign aid, U.S. financial support that provides a buffer against disaster, or better, that boosts an economy to a threshold beyond which it can fend for itself, is a wise investment. The point is not to buy off an elite or to sell U.S. products but to alter basic economic policies of other states.

Here a problem arises. On the one hand, the absolute amount of money provided may be far less important than how the U.S. government conditions and targets its use. On the other hand, financial assistance has taken on a symbolic importance; unless Washington coughs up large sums, it is deemed not serious about helping the new democratic government. This is a trap, and it needs to be forthrightly rejected. Also, it is not always easy to tell when fragile Latin democracies are sincere about restructuring, or are merely seeking new ways to extract funds from U.S., Japanese, and West European banks. If they are not sincere, then lenders will find themselves in the position of a child who discovers too late that the string looped around his finger is not attached to the axle of his yo-yo.

Haiti after the fall of Jean-Claude Duvalier is an example of the political importance of aid. After Duvalier fled, the U.S. government promised a considerable amount of economic aid to Haiti in the hopes that it would prod the democratic process. But the government of Henri Namphy systematically used the money to its own private advantage, leading to the suspension of virtually all the funds. At one point, the Haitian government held tainted elections in which Leslie Manigat emerged victorious. Manigat tried, under extremely difficult circumstances, to expand the prospect for real democracy in the future. To this end, he pleaded with the U.S. government to resume aid, lest Washington's refusal be used by his enemies against him. The U.S. government withheld aid and, partly as a result, Manigat was overthrown. He might also have failed with the aid too, but his chances were reduced sharply without it.

Use U.S. influence to keep the military in the barracks.

Democracy cannot emerge in many countries because the military will not let it. In those cases — and there are exceptions — wherever it can, and when democratization is the objective, the United States government must try to encourage the professional and proper military etiquette that befits a democracy. This is sometimes hard to do because arms transfers from the United States may be required for other purposes, like fighting an insurgency. As noted above, the problem here is to distinguish between aid levels that meet legitimate needs for defense and those that enable military institutions to thwart progress toward democracy. Since the same weapons in different hands can be used for both things, this is a problem that never goes away. Clearly, sending weapons for use against an insurgency does not insure that democracy in all its splendor will burst forth, free of all the limitations of a country's history and culture. But as the case of El Salvador has shown, democracy will certainly not flourish if the insurgency waxes, or if it should take power — but it *might* make some progress if the insurgency is beaten back.

The U.S. government has other means besides arms supplies for leverage. It can also play an important role counselling — or in some cases threatening — the militaries in new democracies to stay out of politics. In 1978, it pointedly warned the Dominican Republic's military that its intervention against an elected government would lead to a complete aid cutoff. The threat had the intended effect. In Peru in 1987 and 1988, and in Guatemala in 1987, U.S. pressure effectively prevented or inhibited military coups against elected governments.

And, in addition, programs that bring officers to the United States for military training help professionalize the militaries of young democracies and make them aware of the benefits of civilian rule. To refine and expand these programs is a worthwhile investment. Clearly, if the U.S. government chooses or is forced to terminate its military-to-military institutional relations, its benign influence is terminated, too, and other indisputably less benign influences take its place. When the U.S. military abandoned Chile during the Pinochet period, it was largely replaced by that of South Africa.

Celebrate the new democrat . . .

Washington needs to acclaim new democrats and give them moral support. President Reagan did it right on his trip to Latin America in 1982. He chose to visit only two countries, one democracy (Colombia) and one country in transition to democracy (Brazil). He visited no dictatorships. In 1985-86, the presidents of ten new democracies were invited to the United States for state visits; the leaders of dictatorships were pointedly excluded. At the United Nations, Secretary of State George Shultz emphasized the comity of U.S. relations with Latin democracies, but not dictatorships.

This pattern broke down the Latin American myth that Washington prefers Latin dictatorships to democracies. It also defanged Congressional opposition to a number of the administration's policies — like continued aid to El Salvador and Honduras at fairly high levels. It was right, and it was effective.

. . . But be patient with those moving ahead more slowly.

Democracy is more than an idea; working democracies function because they are institutionally solid. Overthrowing tyrants, and even arranging free elections, are easy things to do compared to institutionalizing political pluralism and the rule of law where it has not existed in strength. As Stephen Bosworth, U.S. ambassador in the Philippines between 1984 and 1987, explains: "The United States has to be prepared to be patient. We don't always recognize that what's involved is the building of institutions. It's a time consuming process. You have to be prepared to accept reverses. It's not a smooth road of success after success."[3] So as long as the general direction of political development is positive, there is hope.

Bosworth might have added that it's not a smooth road of failure after failure, either. When it looked as though Haiti could sink no further under General Prosper Avril — a man who, along with Henri Namphy, had made the overthrow of Jean-Claude Duvalier in 1986 seem like so much wasted effort — the Haitian people rose up, and at least created some light at the end of the tunnel where there seemed to be none. On March 10, 1990, Avril resigned and the next day, in what is coming to be a Haitian custom, boarded a U.S. C-140 for exile in the United States. Haiti still has its troubles but, for once perhaps, things might be looking up. Certainly, the election of Rev. Jean-Bertrand Aristide in December 1990, his protection against perfidy by, of all parties, the Haitian armed forces, and his relatively trouble free inauguration in February 1991 are reasons for hope. If Haiti can do it, any country can.

Notes

1   See Stephen Van Evera, "The Case Against Intervention," *The Atlantic Monthly*, July 1990, p. 76, who (erroneously) thinks the United States was clearly guilty in all these cases and more besides.
2   These ideas derive in part from Morton Kondracke, "How to Save Democracies," *The New Republic*, December 22, 1986.
3   Quoted in David Hoffman, "How Can U.S. Foster Newborn Democracies?" *The Washington Post*, February 27, 1990.

4　Chastise with Care

We should not hurry, we should not be impatient, but we should confidently obey the eternal rhythm.

— Nikos Kazantzakes,
Zorba the Greek

Keep history in mind when making moral judgments about a Friendly Tyrant. Be gentler with the improving autocrat than with the lapsed democrat. Do not assume either that everyone loves democracy or that even most authoritarian political culture is trapped forever in cycles of repression and revolt. All government is capable of both retrogression and improvement.

Do not project American standards and values onto other countries.
Even though they usually know better upon reflection, Americans tend to think that the world is an enlarged version of the United States. It is commonly believed that foreigners may have unpronounceable names and speak in unintelligible tongues but, deep down, everyone in every country is basically the same. Given half a chance, no one will refuse a ranch house and baseball, or, as Francis Fukuyama put it: "We might summarize the content of the universal homogeneous state as liberal democracy in the political sphere combined with easy access to VCRs and stereos in the economic."[1]

This assumption leads to a second-natured predisposition to apply political metaphors and symbols of American life to other peoples. Specialists usually know enough to beware of such assumptions, but the average person, the average politician, and even the average American president usually does not.

This projection of American standards has many implications for the Friendly Tyrants dilemma. Most Americans reason that if these fellows are so beloved by their people, as they almost always claim, then why fear the result of an election? Since Americans assume that everyone values democracy and political liberty as they do, it follows that dictators can never be really popular and thus must always rule by coercive means.

This happens not to be true, however. Most dictators cultivate constituencies and these allow them to rule by means other than coercion. At the beginnings of their political careers, some dictators — Batista, Trujillo, Franco — were very popular. Others remained popular throughout, like the irascible Juan Perón of Argentina. Americans cannot understand it when Guatemalans yearn for General Ríos Montt, the very tyrant that had to be "retired" for elections to take place.

Other cultures may also lack the American abhorrence of violence by authorities. One reason has to do with fear of the unknown. As a Muslim saying puts it, "Tyranny is better than anarchy." Another is the machismo of many cultures, not only Latin American ones, in which the abilities to inflict and to suffer pain are deemed signs of virile manhood (or of saintliness, in the case of the latter). Thirdly, in many societies, even some democratic ones, government is understood as a form of paternal authority on a larger level. As a father rightfully disciplines a child, so a government may rightfully discipline its people. Even though most Americans find such attitudes almost incomprehensible, they exist just the same. Certainly, they exist in Kuwait and Saudi Arabia, whereas Western notions of legitimate authority do not.

Graft and corruption are more tolerated elsewhere, too. Americans tend to have a puritanical view of how public servants should behave, so much so that an admission by Jimmy Carter that he "lusted in his heart" after attractive women became a major issue in his 1976 campaign for the presidency. (One can only imagine what French politicos made of this.) Americans incline to see high levels of corruption as symptoms of a crisis in other countries. Not so; corruption sometimes serves as a political grease that lubricates the wheels of a rigid system. In Mexico, the ruling PRI party is mass-based not in the sense that grassroots activism can change government policy, but in the top-down sense that gift money is distributed in proportion to, and as a sign of, one's position in the social hierarchy. The trickle-down of money drawn from the public trough at various levels sates the anger of those without access to real power, and allows the system to straggle on.

In Indonesia, China, Japan, and Korea, it is common to give substantial gifts to business associates. The distinction between business activity and social activity is not nearly so clear as it is in the United States. As part of the culture, such gift giving is a necessary element of smooth business life. To Americans doing business in such environs, these practices often appear as nothing less than extortion.

Corruption acquires political importance only when local standards are exceeded, and one must know the culture to know what those are. Anastasio Somoza's venality did not hurt him until his outrageous thievery of international earthquake aid after 1972. When politicians in Zaire steal according to their rank, it is as normal in that country as management consultants are in the United States. Getting rich in public life is considered normal in the Philippines, but the Marcos family violated expected levels of wealth by several orders of magnitude.

Don't rely on metaphors drawn from the American experience to understand other peoples' problems.

Americans carry over some metaphors from U.S. political life to foreign cultures. This attitude comes very naturally; it is also invariably mistaken.

The U.S. racial experience provides a prism that is applied, almost without change, to the situation in South Africa. The tone of the American discussion of South Africa bears the unmistakable cadences of domestic racial problems and tensions. Gold mines become cotton plantations, apartheid becomes Jim Crow, Soweto becomes Selma, Nelson Mandela becomes Martin Luther King Jr., the African National Congress becomes the NAACP, and disinvestment becomes civil rights marching. The fact that none of these pairs match means that American foreign policy marches to its own drummer, with minimal reference to the events or dynamics in South Africa. South Africa functions as a passion play for Americans who are more interested in their own country than in South Africa. Yet the acting out of this passion play has consequences for U.S. foreign policy, as shown in 1986 by the sanctions imposed by the U.S. Congress.

Americans easily understand civil antagonisms abroad when they are defined by skin color, as with black against white in South Africa. They have more trouble understanding antagonisms among language/culture groupings when members of those groups have the same skin color. Unless they attain specific knowledge of such antagonisms, Americans assume that Xhosa and Zulu peoples, both being "black," share similar views about their situation in South Africa. Of course, they do not, and have fought each other over their considerable differences. To them, language/culture differences are seen to be as important as racial differences are to Americans.

Another example concerns the American assumption that military intervention in politics is always bad. We keep our military out of politics and are proud of it, assuming that military participation in government is somehow inherently antidemocratic. But this is not always so. Many

Americans assume that Turkey is a Friendly Tyrant because the military plays such an important role. But, hard as it is for most Americans to grasp, the Turkish military was the midwife of Turkish democracy and remains its protector. The same may be said to a different degree about the role of the military in the Republic of China on Taiwan.

Yet another assumption Americans make is that all democracies have elections and all countries that have real elections are ipso facto democracies. Elections are important, to be sure. But behind American elections stand real parties, real constituencies, real interests, and real philosophical differences. In many Latin American countries, no mass based parties exist and elections really take place only within a very limited political class. This is one reason why Latin democracies have proved so fragile over the years and have often returned to Friendly Tyrants status — as Argentina has over the years; they have the forms of democracy but much of the time, unfortunately, lack the substance.

Don't try to turn every story into a two-sided conflict, because not every conflict has good guys and bad guys — or even better and worse guys — from the American point of view.

Americans search for good guys — moderates, pragmatists, doves, centrists — in even the most unfriendly governments. When none turn up, Washington has an unfortunate tendency to invent them, out of whole cloth if need be. The tendency to reify these labels can generate dangerous misperceptions.

In 1977-79, the Carter administration believed that somewhere, somehow, there had to be good guys in the Nicaraguan political arena. Somoza was bad, as were the Sandinistas, so the "Center," deemed a stable, powerful, moderate and democratic force, was postulated as the savior. But there was no such stable and powerful Center; and to the extent it did exist, U.S. policy unwittingly weakened it by failing to get rid of Somoza in an expeditious way. By the time Somoza fell, most of what had made up the Center had by then made its deal with the Sandinistas in hopes of moderating and ultimately outlasting them. But the Sandinistas, as a Leninist vanguard party, always had the advantage in that regard, and they won out. The Reagan administration divided the Iranian leadership into "moderates" and "militants" in the mid-1980s, and made policy accordingly. In fact, there were only militants; they divided only into tactical militants and irrational militants.

At times, distinctions much finer than "good" and "bad" become critical. Disgusted and disheartened by the travesty of violence in Haiti,

American opinion looked upon the 1986 elections as unholy. Most candidates were banned by the military and the election itself was neither fair nor open. But, despite the American skepticism, the victor, Leslie Manigat, was not just another ravenous opportunist or creature of the military. Working with him and helping him widen his room to maneuver might have prevented his overthrow and Haiti's descent into yet a lower level of political depravity under Prosper Avril. Instead, the U.S. government withheld aid, the Congress bickered, and the lobbies complained. Before anyone realized what had happened, the opportunity was lost.

For a foreign political conflict to seize the American consciousness, it has to break down into two teams. Americans tend to lose their bearings in a three-sided or four-sided conflict; interest in such a conflict will wane. This leads to a misguided tendency to squeeze the parties into a two-team paradigm.

Americans were befuddled when it turned out that the main threat to the shah of Iran came not from the Left but from the religious Right. In South Africa, divisions go far beyond black and white. There are Afrikaners and English speakers; coloreds and Asians; Xhosa, Zulu, and many other tribes; and a host of political factions and organizations.

Don't assume that everyone loves democracy . . .

Hard as it is for Americans to get it through their heads, the American form of democracy does not appeal to all peoples. America is the first and most important democratic mass society in history; it also has a presidential as opposed to a parliamentary form of democracy. Even those disposed toward democracy might well prefer European forms to the American one. More to the point, however, not all societies are disposed toward democracy in any form at all.

Even though democracy's general appeal is increasing rapidly in our time, it is not without strong enemies. Religious fanaticism militates against democracy, for one thing. Algeria is a democracy of sorts as of this writing, but it probably will not be one for long, for fundamentalist Muslims won. Otherwise, there are no serious religious regimes anywhere that are democracies. If people believe that God is on their side and only their side, they are under no obligation to be tolerant.

The martial spirit of patriarchal authority is not conducive to democracy either. Nationalism can be abused, and frequently has been abused. And perduring poverty often banishes thoughts of democracy from the mind altogether.

Trujillo, Batista, Salazar, and Franco were downright popular figures before they became greedy, or corrupt, or brutal, or just old and unattractive. So, in more recent times, to the astonishment of many congressmen, was Zia al-Haq of Pakistan.

Zaireans might like democracy if they had time to think about it. But except for rare occasions, and certain small groups of people, they don't have time — they are too busy surviving, and trying to build an educational system that can produce a population that is more than 20 percent literate.

It's important to get this straight. The United States cannot make people more democratic than they themselves wish or are able to be; this has been the U.S. problem in places like Argentina for most of the last forty years. Most of us fervently believe that whenever people are free to choose, they choose to be free as we understand the term. But it's not always so.

Nor should the United States overestimate how much so-called or would-be democrats will sacrifice for their beliefs in a pinch. Many Reagan administration officials thought that Panama's Civic Crusade represented a true welling up of native enthusiasm for democracy. A coup was encouraged in March 1988 based partly on the belief that the Civic Crusade would finish the job. When General Noriega's Dignity Battalions hit the streets, however, the Civic Crusade blew away like so many dry leaves in December. So did the coup attempt. The fact that the great majority of Panamanians supported the U.S. ouster of Noriega a few months later does not change the fact that Panamanians failed to act on their own behalf, and probably bodes ill for the stability of democratic government in that country in the future.

. . . But never assume that a country is doomed forever to be non-democratic.

The U.S. government has concluded on a number of occasions that democracy cannot succeed in a country, leading to a lack of interest in supporting political reforms. While it is true that some political cultures are more compatible with full democracy than others, it is a mistake to give up on anyone. Things change: countries with a long history of repression can very quickly learn democratic ways. Germans and Japanese produced two of the most horrible governments of the century, then became model democrats (quickly in the case of West Germans, forty-five years later in the case of East Germans). China hands assured us that the Chinese have no interest in democracy; and then, overnight, the Goddess of Democracy sprang up in Tiananmen Square. We learn from this that any political culture, even the most resistant to democracy, can be improved.

Such prejudices against hope have special importance vis-à-vis Friendly Tyrants. In 1974, Henry Kissinger held that Greece was prone to authoritarianism; when the junta fell, Washington expected soon to be dealing with another group of colonels, so it did not warmly congratulate the new democratic government. Lack of U.S. confidence in a newly democratic Greece set an unnecessarily cool tone for relations with the democratic governments that followed.

In the same year, Kissinger gave up on Portugal. But, happily, the U.S. ambassador there and West European Social Democrats did not.

In Haiti, the judgment that democracy was foreign to the political culture was true enough, but a level of basic civil decency well short of democracy nonetheless may protect the country from still further descent into the political hell that, when advanced enough, inevitably becomes a problem for the U.S. government. While nothing the U.S. government might have done in the 1970s could have brought democracy to Haiti, some of the catastrophes of the 1980s might have been avoided had U.S. policy reflected a more serious effort to monitor and complain about the advanced deterioration of the legal system and instruments of economic management. But it didn't, and now Father Aristide has proven that the effort might not have been in vain.

The Middle East, along with sub-Saharan Africa, has a strange place in American thinking. Although the general tendency is to expect everyone to love democracy — which is quite wrong, as noted above — few Americans expect anything from Friendly Tyrants ruling in Morocco, Tunisia, Egypt, Sudan, Saudi Arabia, and Oman, despite the serious human rights abuses that occur in most of these countries. On the other hand, Americans have distinct, even shrill concerns about human rights in the region's few democracies — Israel, Turkey, and (sometimes) Pakistan. This isn't fair, but it is a fact.

Hold authoritarian allies to their own standards; the more democratic they say they are, the higher the standard to which you should hold them.

Hypocrisy is often the advanced wave of a new truth. Vestigial constitutions in lapsed democracies offer the U.S. government fragile but real instruments to encourage democracy. That the Philippines under Marcos in 1986 had a meaningful constitution provided Washington with a lever that does not exist in such countries as Zaire, Somalia, or Saudi Arabia. When governments pronounce themselves fully in favor of human rights, and accept the responsibilities of the United Nations charter, we know that they are often cynical. But unless we try, at least, to hold them to their word, we not only allow their cynicism a free ride, we degrade the charters and normative standards of international life, frail though they may be, even further.

By extension, the pious charters of "revolutionary" anti-American dictatorships, filled with high-sounding but contentless paeans to the rights of the people, can also play a positive role. The Sandinistas in Nicaragua issued many high-sounding declarations and, by doing so, they allowed an atmosphere to develop wherein U.S. demands for a free election were more difficult to fob off — although they certainly tried. That, in turn, allowed the Nicaraguan people a chance to express their views and the result was a victory for democracy.

Support indigenous elements seeking legal remedies and legal reform.

Again in the Philippines, the U.S. government associated itself with domestic constituencies seeking an investigation of Benigno Aquino's assassination, and with those wishing to insure fairness in the 1986 presidential election. For Americans to have pursued these objections on their own would not only have been harder, it would have bruised nationalist sensitivities even in a land characterized by a special U.S.-Filipino relationship.

Even in the absence of democratic politics, constitutional and legal reform have utility. In more homely terms, one must take off one's shoes before one can take off one's socks. Tyrants sometimes wish to constitutionalize their dictatorships in hopes of legitimizing their rule, even though so doing may actually undermine that legitimacy. Constitutional formalism partly explains how Franco unwittingly prepared the way for democracy after his death. In Chile, a poorly calculated attempt at constitutional manipulation in 1986 led to Pinochet's defeat in a plebiscite in October 1988. A constitution would have built expectations for a fair election in Haiti in late 1986 or 1987 and provided the country's few democrats something to hold on to.[2] These days, it is very good that there is pressure on the al-Sabah family to reinstitute the Kuwaiti constitution.

Push harder for democracy in fair weather than in foul.

Pressures for democracy must be connected to specific political conditions. Neglecting facts on the ground makes the U.S. government at best irrelevant, at worst a source of damage. Pressure for democracy should be exerted in relatively calm times, when a little trouble whets the appetite for reform. On a calm day, the fair breeze of democracy can send the sloop sailing away from the putrid odor of dictatorship; in a gale, however, it might swamp the boat and send it under.

After General Zine El Abidine Ben Ali of Tunisia overthrew the aged Habib Bourguiba in 1987, he promised an election. It came in April 1989, but was arranged in such a way that only the ruling Constitutional Democratic party won seats. The U.S. government, acting in unison with Paris, might have pressed Tunis to really make good on its promises. Alas, it did not.

Egypt has deep economic problems which will not be solved until Hosni Mubarak removes the group of military-bureaucratic dead-beats that did so much to create them in the first place. The U.S. government often makes this argument in Cairo, but Mubarak hesitates. Still, U.S. pressure does move him along a little, and that is to the good. Egypt's political strength after the Gulf war should provide the occasion for more careful U.S. pressure, too.

Corazon Aquino of the Philippines also faces immense economic troubles, plus a Marxist-Leninist insurgency; neither will be solved unless the inbred cronyism and grotesquely unequal distribution of land in the Philippines is altered. The time to press this point is before things get out of hand.

Daniel Arap Moi should be pressed sooner rather than later to stop tampering with basic liberties in Kenya, even within the context of that one-party system. In another few years, he will not be able to listen even if he wants to.

Andrés Rodríguez in Paraguay needs to be reminded of the need to live up to his campaign promises after he overthrew General Alfredo Stroessner. The political culture undergirding democracy in Paraguay is much too fragile to let the general stray. So far so good, more or less, but so far isn't yet very far.

Do not even contemplate dissuading a state from pursuing its vital interests.

A ruler who feels its vital interests to be threatened will suspend liberties and freedoms in the effort to survive. Indeed, as Oliver Wendell Holmes noted, a democracy is not obligated to allow the willful misuse of democratic freedoms to undermine that democracy. Even the United States, with all its advantages, has had recourse to exceptional, and sometimes very unfortunate, measures such as the interning of American citizens of Japanese ancestry during World War II "just in case." If the U.S. government resorts to such practices, then surely other states will, too.

It was unrealistic to expect full democracy in the midst of the Vietnamese civil war. Saigon could not maintain Westminister rules so long as the country had to contend with a vicious insurgency. José Napoleon Duarte and Alfredo Cristiani have done pretty much all that they reasonably could be expected to do in El Salvador under the circumstances. Peru's government, threatened by the Sendero Luminoso and a parlous economic situation on its doorstep, cannot be expected to expand its fragile democracy in a way that impedes the anti-insurgency struggle.

By the same token, Washington could not in all fairness demand fully democratic elections in Nicaragua while the country was still reeling from a civil war largely supported by the U.S. government. After the government's ceasefire with the rebels and the suspension of lethal aid from the United States to the contras, however, it could and did.

Do not preach.

Politicians and diplomats need to be sensitive not only to what Americans say to other peoples, but also how they say it. This is especially important because Americans, when they speak about politics abroad, tend to get moralistic. This is counterproductive and unwarranted. Other peoples resent being lectured at by Americans about as much as Americans resent being lectured at by Indians and Swedes. In retrospect, this may well have been President Carter's greatest tactical error — the tone more than the content of what he said.

The imposition of sanctions against South Africa was accompanied by an embarrassingly self-righteous rhetoric. Speaker after speaker bore witness before Congress, invoking the sufferings and sacrifices of those who participated in the civil rights movement as a mandate from which to lecture other peoples. In fact, the air of condescension and hostility was particularly inappropriate for the United States where, a mere thirty years earlier, Jim Crow flourished literally within sight of the Lincoln Memorial. Americans, understandably, have been quick to forget such hurtful things — amnesia is healing. But peoples in other countries have not forgotten.

Notes

1 Francis Fukuyama, "The End of History?" *The National Interest*, Summer 1989, p. 8.
2 Haitians finally got a Constitution in 1987 and, without it, the December 1990 elections, the first free and fair elections in Haitian history, probably could not have been held.

5 Define Goals

If you don't know where you're going, most any road will take you there.

— Lewis Carroll,
Alice in Wonderland

Establish and prioritize goals. In normal times, the appropriate goal is to build a stable relationship with a country that can outlast any particular regime. In crises, the goal is to preserve U.S. interests. The mere retention or removal of a dictator is not a suitable goal.

Do not allow policy to become personalized around a dictator.

Dictators are often interesting people. But they are not so interesting that their personalities should be allowed to obscure the range of U.S. interests. When the U.S. government becomes preoccupied with a personality, other facets of policy get less attention than they deserve.

This is especially the case when the tyrant becomes target. In 1961, getting rid of Trujillo was an *idée fixe* in the Kennedy administration, to the point that a plan for the transition after him was almost an afterthought. Not surprisingly, the transition was botched. Getting rid of President Diem became an obsession — to the exclusion of considering what would follow him. The same applied to Somoza in the Carter administration. When it came to Manuel Noriega, President Bush may have been guilty of an *idée fixe* although, in fairness, he was egged on by Democrats in Congress to act boldly. He openly admitted his frustration with Noriega, but following the invasion, it became clear that the administration had no plans readied for economic recovery, reconstitution of the defense forces, or practically anything.

Ignore cheering squads within the United States, either for the opposition or for the dictator.

No matter who they are and what they stand for, opponents of Friendly Tyrants can find influential supporters in the United States. Castro had

Herbert Matthews at *The New York Times*. Andrew Young informed Americans that Khomeini was "a saint," while some Iranian experts assured Americans that the religious leaders there "would never participate directly in the formal governmental structure."[1] Liberals and some foreign service officers declared in 1979 that Washington could work with the Sandinistas. Today, there are at least some American boosters who celebrate the ANC, Kurds seeking to destabilize the Turkish Republic, native Taiwanese who oppose mainlander dominance, East Timorians and South Mollucans who oppose Indonesian occupation, the New Peoples Army in the Philippines, and the Chilean far Left.

These boosters deserve a hearing for informational purposes, but no more. Some are paid agents, some are confused, others are committed ideologically to movements that hurt the United States. Groups espousing such views need to be carefully tracked by scholars and commentators; however marginal in the normal course of events, they gain prominence and credibility when crisis strikes.

As for the American friends of dictators, they deserve roughly the same treatment. Shah-boosters in the United States announced that the shah would turn Iran into the world's fifth industrial power and the Switzerland of the Middle East. Greece offers a particularly vivid example of intelligence agency clientitis. Marcos, Somoza, Batista, Chiang Kai-shek, Rhee, Park, Diem, all had U.S. boosters in Congress and elsewhere. Diem, for example, carefully cultivated the major personalities in the Catholic archdiocese in New York City, and when the Kennedy administration came into office in January 1961, this conduit proved to be of special utility to him.

Nothing can be done about Friendly Tyrants' boosters; the Constitution allows them to exist and they will continue to make noise because they benefit in one way or another. For registered foreign agents, it is their business to make such noises.[2] But there is no reason for serious analysts to pay attention to their advocacy.

Don't let stability become an end in itself.

Stability should never become the only U.S. policy goal concerning a Friendly Tyrant. U.S. foreign policy has no business supporting the stability of the grave, of the gulag, of the political prison anywhere. That is the sort of "stability" that has been supported traditionally by the Soviet Union and its allies, pretensions to progressiveness notwithstanding. Although there are times when the U.S. government should and must live with less in an ally, it should be fully satisfied only with a dynamic stability, a stability that is solid because it marks steady progress. We want nothing less for our own country, so why necessarily think in terms of less for other countries?

The promotion of political pluralism is clearly worth some decline in stability, but there is a limit set by prudence. If the promotion of political pluralism is fatal to the regime and benefits anti-American forces, then prudent limits have been exceeded. Admittedly, this is a tricky business because the balance between prudence and heavy-handedness is ever elusive. But sometimes seeing this balance is easier. When stability resides in one person (King Hussein in Jordan has been a case in point), it usually constitutes a formula for trouble somewhere down the road. Single-minded U.S. devotion to stability led to policies that contributed to unnecessarily polarized politics in the Philippines, Greece, and South Korea. In Egypt today, that government's extraordinary economic problems are used as an excuse to leave off encouraging the liberalizing tendencies of the Mubarak regime. To the contrary: troubled times are often required for basic reform, for the regime has no motivation to take risks in stable times. The Kennedy administration's support for social reform in Iran in was wise and more effective than often is recognized.

Quite aside from money, there is also the matter of liberty. Stability in places like Zaire and Indonesia means a denial of liberty and basic human rights. To recognize this is not only disheartening, but also raises a practical question: how long will it be before people deprived of their rights rise up and seize them? It may be a long time in some cases . . . but it won't be forever.

As a Friendly Tyrant's life cycle advances, decide as early as possible on the basis of U.S. interests if and when to abandon reform and seek to remove a tyrant.

Promoting instability must be done with extreme care. From the start, the U.S. government must be clear within its own councils to what purpose it contemplates pressuring a regime — whether to reform or eliminate a tyrant. If the aim is reform, the tyrant must be asked to do things he can in fact do. If the aim is removal, then press him with stark alternatives and go after his essential support structures. When he resists, do what you must to weaken the regime fatally. The point is to know very clearly what you are aiming to accomplish before you start the process.

The Carter administration's eleventh hour starving of Somoza's National Guard is a casebook study of what not to do. The Guard was known to be Somoza's major prop in 1978-79, so depriving it of weapons was designed to bring down Somoza's regime and replace it with a centrist government. Of course, for this plan to succeed, a centrist government had to come into existence before the Sandinistas grabbed power — but to expect this was the sheerest wishful thinking. Everyone makes tactical mistakes. In this case, even taking this chance in a minor suit would have been justified if Washington had been prepared to pull trump, i.e., to intervene to put things right if things went wrong. But the Carter administration was not, and found itself hopelessly trying to "reconstruct" the Guard in Somoza's final days as a buffer between the old and new regimes. This unwillingness to pull trump is what turned a forgivable mistake into an unjustifiable risk. The moral: do not drain the swimming pool before closing the diving board.

In contrast, escalating U.S. pressures on Ferdinand Marcos in 1985, which ultimately led him to call elections in early 1986 as a way to sidestep these pressures, was done on the basis of more or less known quantities — Corazon Aquino and Salvador Laurel — and so made good sense.

If you choose reform, effectiveness will depend on leaving a tyrant a clear way to reduce U.S. pressures.

If the aim is to reform a regime before it undermines itself, the United States government must leave the tyrant an explicit way out, without an undue loss of his prestige, or reforms will be stymied. Do not push for reforms that undermine a tyrant's core political base, or he will resist the reforms with all he has, leading to deadlock.

In the Philippine case, for example, U.S. diplomats — Stephen Bosworth, Michael Armacost, Richard Armitage, Paul Wolfowitz — were always careful to let Marcos know exactly what he could do to relieve U.S. pressures on him. Purge corrupt army officers, for example. Restore the integrity of the legal process, for another. That Marcos did not avail himself of these "outs" was a measure of his miscalculation. In the end, Marcos decided on an election — which he was sure he could win — as a way to relieve the pressure. He lost the election, bungled an attempt to rig the results, and so undid himself in the eyes of his own people. This made his removal infinitely easier than if the United States had had to see to it more directly. That is largely why the Philippine episode was so successful from the U.S. point of view.

Do not undermine a Friendly Tyrant unless you are sure the alternative will be better.

Before contemplating the overthrow of a tyrant, be very sure you know beforehand that what will follow represents an improvement. Don't fall for the idea that "things can't get worse." Yes, they can get worse and, what's more, they often do.

The sad circus of Big Minhs and Little Minhs following President Ngo Dinh Diem was much, much worse than what preceded. Castro has been worse than Batista. The Sandinistas were worse than Somoza. Khomeini was worse than the shah. Even Henri Namphy and Prosper Avril have by many measures been worse for Haiti even than "Baby Doc" Duvalier, hard as that is to imagine. When an unnamed expert says that "Whoever it is will have to work pretty damn hard to be worse than [Siad] Barre [of Somalia],"[3] he is probably wrong, too — although as of this writing the dust has yet to settle in that unhappy land. Nothing is so ugly that something else can't be uglier. In many cases, better the devil you know than the one you don't.

Should you choose removal over reform, do not usurp the opposition by declaring an all-out campaign to oust a Friendly Tyrant.

The expectation of U.S. support is usually a source of encouragement to opposition movements such as the Partido Acción Nacional (PAN) in Mexico, Argentines under the junta, and the Chilean opposition between 1985 and 1988. And that is good. Unless some support is given, the perception that the U.S. government have given a carte blanche to a ruler can cause the opposition to despair. This was true for a time in the Philippines and Iran (mainly in the 1970s). It is true today in Zaire and Indonesia.

But democratic oppositions must never be given the impression that the U.S. government will do their work for them, and then hand them power on a platter. After the return of two federal indictments against Manuel Noriega in February 1988, the Reagan administration embarked on a campaign to oust Noriega that displaced the local opposition and drove it to near oblivion. Later, during the May 1989 crisis, touched off when Noriega rigged the Panamanian elections and attacked the opposition candidates, President Bush allowed his rhetoric to outdistance U.S. government planning and commitment. So when Panamanian rebels in October 1989 accused the U.S. government of urging them on against Noriega, only to let them down in the pinch, they had a point.

Here, as in many other instances, the U.S. government must walk a fine line in casting an impression, neither ignoring the aspirations of beleaguered democrats or acting as though Washington will redeem them from folly and indolence. As James Thurber put it, "You might as well fall flat on your face as lean over too far backward."

Worry more about major countries than minor ones . . .

The bigger Friendly Tyrants — China and Iran in the past, Egypt, South Africa, Indonesia, Mexico in the future — have caused or will cause the most trouble for U.S. foreign policy; there is no doubt about it. Everyone assumes that such countries will absorb the attention of any administration tasked with their management, and rightly so. As it is said: "The bigger they are, the harder they hit."

This piece of advice may seem too obvious to warrant mentioning. And we could do very well without mentioning it except for one thing: the larger and more geostrategically significant a country is to the United States, the harder it seems to be for Washington to formulate a coherent policy. Washington argued bitterly over South Vietnam, nearly paralyzed itself dealing with the Greek junta, and foundered over the Iranian crisis. But Cuban policy, thirty years ago thought to be unimportant, was dispatched easily by a half dozen senior officials, and Batista folded up and left with a minimum of fuss. In Haiti in 1986, U.S. action was bold, rapid, and successful.

Why is this? Because major countries tend to be better known than minor ones, they are more complex, the policy stakes in them are higher, and the number of actors wanting to influence policy is greater. The collision of ideological proclivities and bureaucratic interests tends to be more bitter. A handful of specialists make policy toward Somalia; the whole country seems to have an opinion on South Africa. All this leads to paralysis when action is most needed.

The Iranian case is vivid in the light it throws here on the difficulty of managing the big ones. Everyone in the Carter administration knew that Iran was important. And few administration principals assumed blithely that everything would work out for the best. But between pleas for restraint coming from the State Department, contingency planning for intervention in the Defense Department, the Commerce Department's ideas about how to preserve American business interests, intelligence wars among the various responsible agencies over what was really going on, and mixed expert opinion on how the revolution would eventually settle, the White House was paralyzed. Everyone voiced an opinion, the Congress was animated, the press was seething. With that many actors involved, it is certain that where there's a will, there's a won't. President Carter temporized too long, and policy fell flat on its face. So, in short order, did that president's political career.

Like it or not, Americans cannot slay every monster, nor can they save every sparrow that falls from its nest. Choices have to be made, and when it comes to Friendly Tyrants, that means first and foremost knowing as much as possible about monsters and sparrows.

. . . But don't underestimate the damage that even a "small" Friendly Tyrants crisis can cause.

American policy makers often take small or obscure countries for granted, thinking that their capacity to generate pain is limited. This is dangerously wrong. After all, Fidel and the Sandinistas — very unpleasant and troublesome little regimes — both came into being as the result of a botched Friendly Tyrants crisis. By themselves they could not assault major U.S. interests, true. But they were not by themselves. And besides, what roils the waters of domestic politics in the United States is not necessarily a function of the objective strategic stakes involved in a foreign policy crisis.

Dwight Eisenhower paid little or no attention to Batista until forced by the advanced deterioration of the regime. Until Batista fled, top U.S. officials spent virtually no time thinking about Cuba; none imagined the disruption Fidel Castro would cause within a few years. In Vietnam, the American commitment to South Vietnam was an accumulation of episodic decisions made at a variety of levels over a twenty-year period. Indeed, the Vietnam debacle is the outstanding example of a minor issue turning into a major debacle. The war also caused other problems; top American officials were so immersed for so long in the Vietnam issue, neither the fall of democracy in Greece in 1967 nor its restoration in 1973 attracted serious attention.

After an initial effort to oust Nicaragua's Somoza failed, top officials of the Carter administration were absorbed by SALT II and the Iranian revolution. By the time high level attention turned back to Nicaragua roughly ten months later, the situation on the ground had changed drastically in favor of a Sandinista victory, a fact neither fully appreciated nor adequately planned for by the White House. In Panama, Reagan administration officials made a series of uninformed judgments about the strength of the Civic Crusade and the breadth of General Noriega's constituency.

The United States didn't pay very much attention to Iraqi threats against Kuwait in the summer of 1990; instead, it was fixated on the minutiae of matters Palestinian. What a mistake that was . . .

Little countries can cause enormous trouble if they are close enough, have the wrong allies, have more important friendly neighbors, or have rulers who are creatively defiant. It is sheer hubris to think otherwise. As in children's stories, a little mouse can befriend a lion by removing a thorn from the cat's foot; in real life, little mice can insert thorns, too.

Notes

1 James Bill, "Iran and the Crisis of '78," *Foreign Affairs*, Winter 1978/79, p. 336.
2 See the fascinating article about Edward van Kloberg by Phil McCombs, "Spin Control for the Third World," *The Washington Post*, July 5, 1990.
3 *The Wall Street Journal*, October 23, 1989.

6 Know the Country

*Do not do unto others as you would they should
do unto you. Their tastes may not be the same.*
— George Bernard Shaw

Whatever you wish to do — seek regime reform or a tyrant's removal
— take account of local standards and circumstances. Understand how
local politics work, then match instruments of American leverage with
apt opportunities.

***Keep in mind how unusual the United States is, and therefore how it
must not serve as your template for understanding other countries.***
The United States is an exceptional place, as everything from the
Statue of Liberty to lopsided United Nations votes make clear. Freedom
to Americans may be chaos to other peoples; law and order to them
borders on unacceptable repression to us. The Carter administration's
idea of draft registration raised cries of fascism; the notion of an identity
card raises the hackles of civil libertarians. By contrast, historically, there
seems to be no Russian tyrant that the Russians would not accept, no
authority to whom they would not offer obedience.

Friendly Tyrants offer many intermediate examples. Chile has a much
more deeply rooted democratic tradition than Paraguay or Argentina. At
the moment, all three are democratic, but one suspects that troubles of the
same kind in these three places — say an economic crisis — would put
less severe pressure on new democratic institutions in Chile than in the
other two.

***Do not assume you know the role of the military, the church, or political
parties: study instead.***
Americans tend to assume they know what is good and bad for other
countries, but the world is too diverse for such assumptions to be much

use as substitutes for understanding. The military is not always the enemy of democracy, but is sometimes its protector. Equally, the church can be in league with the tyrant or opposed to him. Land reform, often assumed to be good, can be irrelevant or pernicious. There is simply too much institutional diversity in the world to extrapolate mechanically from some places to others. Different political cultures see things and value things differently.

In Argentina, Chile, and Greece, soldiers have fouled their countries' democratic traditions. Elsewhere, the military is the godfather, even the creator of democracy. In the Turkish case, it served as the very midwife of democracy, then guardian. In Taiwan, too, the military has supported and nurtured democracy.

In some places, the military is highly regarded. Jordan is a country where the military is held in high esteem and cannot be bypassed. To have influence in that country requires good military-to-military relations. The U.S.-Jordanian Joint Military Group that meets each year is one of the most durable bonds of U.S.-Jordanian ties; when Congress cuts U.S. military assistance to Jordan against administration advice, it not only affects military matters, but stabs at the heart of the U.S.-Jordanian bilateral relationship.

Elsewhere, as in Haiti and Zaire, the military is despised for its corruption, violence against civilians, and general ineptitude. When this is the case, a dual strategy is required. In the near term, better to avoid the military and deal with other institutions. At the same time, patient efforts should be made to use military relations with these countries to contribute to the professionalization of their armies.

There are programs in place designed to do precisely this — the International Military Education and Training program, for example — and sometimes they work in the pinch. The Portuguese military in 1974-75, for example, retained enough of its professionalism to prevent disaster. Had the army run.amok with politics, saving the country from Portuguese communists might have proven impossible.

Too, the place of organized religion varies dramatically from country to country. Especially in Franco's Spain, and somewhat less so in Salazar's Portugal, the church was part of the establishment and an essential ingredient in its longevity. In Haiti, it has served as a positive, if erratic, force for change. In Nicaragua, it remains in the opposition, contributing in the 1970s to the anti-Somoza forces and to the anti-Sandinista coalition.

Invoke sanctions only when confident they will change either the leadership or the policies of the country in question for, otherwise, they will be counterproductive.

The record shows that sanctions rarely achieve their ends. They work only under certain conditions, conditions which rarely exist. Sanctions work only if the base is narrow and if it is surgically targeted. What constitutes narrowness in a regime base depends both on objective criterion and on political culture. The effective use of sanctions requires detailed knowledge of the dictator's patronage base and coercive power. If you don't master these, sanctions will almost surely backfire.

Effective sanctions are few and far between. The arms embargo against Batista demoralized him and was important to his downfall. An arms embargo against Somoza helped bring down his regime. The Bolivian regime was brought down by sanctions in 1978, but only because they were decisive, and they were decisive, in part, because they were multilateral.

Examples of counterproductive sanctions are easy to find. Not importing Rhodesian chrome after 1965 failed to deter unilateral independence. Denial of aid to South Vietnam after 1973 was not, formally speaking, a sanction, but it was intended to serve as such for many Congressmen; it only assured the fall of Saigon to the Northern troops. Perversely, the Humphrey-Kennedy amendment to the Defense Authorization bill of 1976, directed against Argentina and Chile, not only did not work, but the sanctions actually helped the Friendly Tyrants regimes of the Argentine junta and Augusto Pinochet, by allowing them to pin their troubles on American intrigues and meddling, thus distracting domestic discontent. Further, both the Argentine and Chilean militaries diversified their weapons suppliers to the point that probably neither will turn to U.S. suppliers for a long time to come. Excessively broad sanctions against Noriega in 1988-89 hurt the Panamanian economy to the point that it required a U.S. occupation after the December 1989 invasion to return the country to normal. The recovery may take years and cost billions in American aid before it's all through.

It should also be noted that one of the most successful Friendly Tyrants operations in recent years — the removal of Ferdinand Marcos from the Philippines in 1986 — did *not* involve the use of sanctions. Only in the very last hours of the Marcos regime did the United States threaten to end U.S. military assistance to the Philippines if the government used force against antigovernment demonstrators. Before that, there had been a few

Congressional initiatives proposing to divert military aid to economic uses. But in fact the United States government never placed itself in default to any aid commitments whatsoever, most of which had been made in conjunction with the 1983 review of U.S. military bases agreement.

Don't forget that the psychological impact of sanctions in the target country is often more important than their practical consequences.

The stoppage of arms shipments did not literally disarm the Cuban or Nicaraguan militaries, nor did financial sanctions break the Bolivian regime, but the perception of loss of favor, in the context of other weakness, did the trick. South African sanctions may be another example. From a narrow economic point of view, they were broadly counterproductive. But because South African whites want so much to be considered part of the West, the moral effects of the sanctions may have outweighed the literal economic effects. Such cases are rare.

Other sanctions worked, but not as intended. Those invoked against the Argentine junta did not weaken the junta, but they may have limited somewhat the scope of the "dirty war." Also, they preserved a favorable image of the United States for the day when democracy was restored. One can argue that sanctions against Somoza worked, for he lost power. But they were so poorly timed, they paved the way for an even worse group to take power. Happy as some of these results are, one must stretch logic beyond the breaking point to make a case for sanctions on the basis of unanticipated effects. This makes no more sense than the irresponsible fathering of children is justifiable on the basis of increasing genetic diversity.

For sanctions to work on the symbolic level, they have to make basic sense.

Sanctions are sometimes not meant or expected to work in a literal sense, but are imposed merely to chastise. This is rarely a good idea. Still, whenever sanctions are employed as symbols, the symbol must at least display a modicum of logic. Sheer petulance hardly serves as a basis of foreign policy.

Examples to the contrary abound. In Greece in 1969, the U.S. government cut off deliveries of large scale military equipment, while keeping up small arms deliveries. This was illogical — a tyrannical government represses its own people with small arms, and defends its frontiers with tanks and armored personnel carriers — but it was politically impossible to impose sanctions in any other way and still convey as powerful a symbolic message.

The banning of ores from the rebel regime of Ian Smith in Rhodesia had a particularly absurd outcome. Having renounced Rhodesian ore, the United States Congress, over the objections of the Nixon administration, turned to the one other major source — the Soviet Union. Not only was the Soviet price higher, but much of the chrome purchased from Moscow had been previously acquired by the Soviets from Ian Smith's Rhodesia!

The Reagan administration invoked the Emergency Powers law against Panama from 1986 on, with the effect that no U.S. business concern in Panama could pay money, including taxes, to the Panamanian government. This crude tool undermined whole sections of the Panamanian economy, hurt the middle class it hoped to support as well as key Panamanian canal employees whose friendship we badly need to preserve, and hardly scratched Noriega and his allies. And the United States got stuck with a bill — according to Panamanian officials installed by the 1989 invasion — of about $1 billion in "reparations." The Panamanian gross domestic product fell by 20 percent in 1988 and lost another 10 percent in 1989. Worse, from a symbolic point of view, these sanctions permitted Noriega to portray Washington as the enemy of Panama, rather than of himself, and even gave some credence to his absurd argument that the real American motive was to renege on the Panama Canal treaties of 1978.

Real expertise is invaluable, so invest in it, acquire it, and use it.

Top American politicians spend most of the time they devote to foreign relations thinking about just a few countries or areas: the Soviet Union, Europe, the Middle East, and for a few years, Vietnam. Everything else in the world is back burner material. As a result, high officials have rarely spent time dealing with Zaire, Pakistan, or Chile. When such countries generate acute crises, these officials usually know much too little to be able to think through the consequences of American actions.

This creates a need for a core of foreign service officers, intelligence operatives, and military officers with thorough knowledge of second- and third-tier countries. This means: a thorough command of history and political culture, command of the written and spoken languages; first-hand experience in the country; and personal familiarity with the decision makers.

The U.S. government has such expertise, but not enough; it needs to build up more. Its relative absence leads to obvious problems. The commitment to Vietnam was made at a time when the government had only three Vietnamese speakers at its disposal. The U.S. government had no idea what to do about Khomeini, it believed that a democratic middle could hold in Nicaragua, and it overestimated the power of the Civic Crusade in Panama in 1988.

In the intelligence agencies, the problem is different; a proliferation of computers and satellites has turned analysts into the slaves of quantitative information. However useful these sources are, they cannot substitute for in-depth knowledge of a culture.

Adjust career patterns in the U.S. government to encourage specialization.

Career patterns in the U.S. government virtually preclude thorough knowledge of a country. As in the American corporate world and elsewhere, the federal government rewards diversity and penalizes specialization. A top-notch analyst of Zaire will not stay with that country for long, but will move on to Japan and then Hungary. Staying with a country year after year, unfortunately, is taken as a sign of dullness, even incompetence.

The practice of moving personnel around is usually justified on the grounds that it serves as an antidote to "localitis," the penchant to advocate the interests of a foreign country rather than those of the United States. The assumption is, keep a diplomat posted in South Korea year after year, and he will lose perspective. But the record does not confirm this assumption.

In truth, personnel sent to a country without prior knowledge tend to succumb more readily to localitis because they lack the ability to work independently and have to trust local informants. Further, they lack the knowledge to stand up against prevailing opinion in that country. The only American ambassador who dared speak out against the Ceaucescu regime, for example, was David Funderburk, an academic specialist on Romania. For his trouble, he was treated to much sneering and condescension by the prestige press and the foreign policy establishment.

Of course, academic expertise will not prevent localitis and clientelism all the time, any more than moving people around will. Moreover, some academic experts are victims of the disease, too. A foolproof cure for localitis is a managerial impossibility. But localitis is a problem that professional mobility has not solved, and will not solve.

Another reason why analysts are moved around so often has to do with the deep American preference for an unbiased observer. An aide to President Woodrow Wilson captured this sense perfectly when he explained why Wilson sent two rank amateurs on a potentially critical mission to the Middle East in 1920: he "felt these two men were particularly qualified to go to Syria because they knew nothing about it."[1]

While not stated so boldly in recent years, the feeling still exists that ignorance implies a lack of prejudice. Of course, the truth is just the reverse; whoever is ignorant of a country relies on his pre-formed opinions far more than the specialist.

Promote nongovernmental exchanges.

The greater the number of alternative power centers in the country, and the greater their level of contact with the outside world, the less likely the Tyrant will succeed in dominating his society. Accordingly, to help steer a country toward democracy, the U.S. government should encourage American voluntary organizations to get involved.

Friendly Tyrants need to be reminded that institutions in their society have links to the outside world. The religious establishment almost always has international links, as do the labor unions and the business community. Churches have been important in Haiti, the Philippines, Nicaragua, and South Africa. Business connections have counted in Panama, Taiwan, and South Korea. In South Africa, the Sullivan Principles stand as an example of what extrinsic pressure can do to penetrate and moderate an authoritarian order; the Slepak Principles offer similar potential for the Soviet Union.

Nongovernmental institutions are better at helping build democratic institutions than is Washington. AFL-CIO support for unions in South Africa, arguably the most positive force in the country for racial integration, has worked to very good effect. The National Endowment for Democracy (NED) has already been an active and positive force advancing democracy in Chile (in 1988) and Paraguay (in 1989). With a larger budget, it could do much more. Together with the AFL-CIO and the media, it could engage in a highly effective campaign to insure civic education, labor rights, and free speech. As an agency that encourages nongovernment involvement in foreign affairs, NED may be the Reagan administration's greatest legacy in foreign policy.

Nongovernmental exchanges are useful in another way too: they expand the reservoir of non-official Americans who know foreign countries. American businessmen are especially important here, because they have special incentive to learn the ways of other countries — or else they won't do very much business there.

U.S. sanctions that obstruct such nongovernmental exchanges play right into the hands of a tyrant looking to expand his dictatorial purview, and so are counterproductive. U.S. sanctions against South Africa have had this effect. This brings us to the next point.

Note

1 *Papers Relating to the Foreign Relations of the United States: The Paris Peace Conference, 1919* (Washington, D.C.: U.S. Government Printing Office, 1942-47), vol. 11, p. 133.

7 | **Think It Through**

It's one thing to burn down the shithouse, another to install plumbing.

— P.J. O'Rourke

Husband policy assets carefully and do not deprive yourself of leverage, even in apparently easy cases. In other words: attend to details; don't make promises or threats you can't keep; avoid open-ended commitments; say whatever you can in private; show no gratuitous enmity; impose sanctions with great caution.

Do not offer a Friendly Tyrant unconditional support, or let him think that he has it, or U.S. efforts to influence that political culture will diminish.

The dictator is at best an instrument of policy, not an end; there are always broader sociopolitical factors that are more important to the advancement of American interests. A Friendly Tyrant must not believe that he has a carte blanche from the U.S. government. And even if he does, he must not know it. He may need to be told the contrary, early and often, and even publicly, too.

The impression of unconditional support allows the Friendly Tyrant to ignore U.S suggestions for domestic political reform. For years, Ferdinand Marcos brushed aside suggestions from U.S. officials that he reform the Philippines' decayed legal and economic institutions. He believed that U.S. bases were too important for the United States to bring real pressure to bear, and he was right. Marcos had noted Washington's meek response to his declaration of martial law in 1972 and came to believe he could do anything and still keep American support. A close personal friendship that developed early in the Reagan administration between the two "first couples" magnified this perception of immunity. When the Reagan administration took office and pressures eased, it reinforced Marcos's sense of indispensability, so much so that when the Reagan administration pressed him hard in late 1984 and 1985, he could not at first believe it.

In Nicaragua, Somoza developed a similar sense of invincibility. So long as he could paint the opposition as communist, he assumed Washington would always back him. So sure was he, he ignored a very different set of signals coming from the Carter administration (including the president's well-publicized scorn for the "inordinate fear of communism"). Somoza remained oblivious to the fact that his trump was played out.

This problem still exists. President Mobutu Sese Seko in Zaire seemed until very recently to be under the impression that his interests are as perfectly harmonious with Washington's today as they were twenty years ago. This is largely because U.S. officials act as though the alternative to Mobutu is chaos, and that the chaos would spread — Zaire is a huge country that borders on nine other states. But it may well be that Mobutu's misrule is instead creating the very chaos the United States wants to avoid; but until Washington conveys this message, Zairian policies will remain virtually oblivious to U.S. desiderata.

Finally, a dictator's willful misrepresentation of his relations with Washington can profoundly influence local images of the United States long into the future, and it can have more impact than the actual record. Even today, U.S. complicity in the April 1967 coup is a staple of Greek common knowledge, though it is wrong. The almost boastful comraderie of U.S. embassy and intelligence personnel with their Greek counterparts has made it virtually impossible to persuade the Greek populace that American officials lacked advance knowledge of the April 1967 colonels' coup.

And finally on this point, the United States went to great trouble and expense to put the al-Sabah family back in Kuwait City, but that should not mean, and has not meant, that the al-Sabah family has a carte blanche to shut down newspapers and to torture and murder its enemies. Happily, the Bush administration struck just about the right tone in the aftermath of the war; it was truly a model of policy prudence and balance.

Remind a recalcitrant Friendly Tyrant that alternative allies exist, or the tyrant's willingness to service U.S. foreign policy needs will wane.

Taking American support for granted usually spells obduracy when it comes to foreign policy, too. In 1959-1960, the U.S. government wanted Rafael Trujillo of the Dominican Republic to join the American effort to isolate Castro. Trujillo refused, fearing Castro more than Eisenhower. As it happened, Trujillo was wrong; he was killed in May 1961 in a conspiracy in which the U.S. government was heavily implicated. Still, his calculus made sense, for the U.S. government, through its ambassador, had persuaded Trujillo that he would never be dumped.

Papa Doc Duvalier toyed with alignment with Castro to squeeze U.S. money out of the Eisenhower administration because he took for granted the utility in Washington of his high anticommunist profile.

The Greek colonels did not worry about the U.S. reaction to their plot for *enossis* (the unification of Cyprus and Greece) in 1974; they had extrapolated U.S. support for the status quo in Greece to support for changing the status quo in Cyprus. For a similar reason, they refused to help the United States resupply Israel in October-November 1973, believing that the U.S. stake in Greece was so extensive that turning down American requests for help would have little negative consequence for them. Similarly, the Argentine generals thought that the U.S. government would accede to their seizure of the Falklands, in part because of the warm personal relations between certain junta leaders and members of the Reagan administration. Both regimes soon learned to their dismay how dead wrong they had been.

A carte blanche also encourages complacency about enemies. South Vietnamese generals aspiring to the palace on occasion saved their firepower against the communists to build a larger following for internal political purposes. The assumption that the Americans would never allow the country to fall fueled this irresponsibility.

The preservation of the Saud family gets confused with support for a government in Riyadh responsive to Western interests; the two are not identical. The U.S. government should not necessarily identify as enemies elements in Arabia that want to replace the semi-totalitarian reign of the Saudis with a government that lets political opinions be expressed, Christians pray openly, and women drive cars.

Mistakes on this score point to the need to be very clear about the lines of mutual interest between the U.S. government and a Friendly Tyrant. Calculations made by others on the basis of what they believe U.S. policy to be can have devastating impact. In neither the Cyprus crisis of 1974 nor the Falklands War of 1982 did the Greek or Argentine governments know for sure that the United States would support their use of force, but U.S. signals were not clear what, if anything, the United States would do to reverse a political *fait accompli* that flowed from the use of force. The governments of Greece and Argentina believed they had a carte blanche, and were wrong. Both miscalculations had the merit of undoing — at the hands of Turkey and Britain, respectively — the tyrants that provoked them, but a lot of innocent people got killed in the process, and the U.S.

government found itself in two crises it just might have been able to prevent.

Do not rule out the use of force or covert operations publicly, pre-emptively, or at all . . .

Force, overt or covert, must always remain under consideration even if it is not actually used. The existence of these options, and occasional use of them, makes it much harder for adversaries to predict U.S. policy in advance, and thus acts as a constraint against bellicose or aggressive behavior by others.

To rule out the use of force publicly and in advance — as the Carter administration did in Iran and Nicaragua, as the Reagan administration did in the initial stages of the Panamanian case, and as President Bush seemed to do the morning after the Iraqi invasion of Kuwait on August 2, 1990 — aids and comforts the enemy. If the ultimate sanction is preemptively dismissed, every form of pressure and sanction below that loses some of its punch.

For example, General Noriega was home free in 1987-88 once he knew (or thought he knew) that force would not be used against him. His bold behavior was almost certainly a result of this gratuitous assurance, and when the Bush administration turned to the Organization of American States for help, an organization that would never approve the use of U.S. military force, he might well have concluded that he had won the war of nerves with Washington. It turned out, of course, that American patience had its limits, but his assessment was not wholly illogical.

. . . But expect unanticipated consequences when using force and stealth.

Do not flinch from using force if use it you must, but know that you risk getting into an open-ended adventure.

Military force and covert operations sometimes do work. In 1965, force prevented the possibility of a leftist government from riding to power in Santo Domingo on the back of Juan Bosch. For years, force prevented the substitute of an unfriendly tyrant for a friendly one in South Vietnam. Covert operations did get rid of Trujillo in the Dominican Republic, and helped Mobutu come to power in Zaire at a time when the alternatives to him appeared far worse.

But the downside is also apparent. The use of force in Vietnam had many unanticipated and unfortunate effects on Southeast Asian and U.S. politics. The failure to win and the failure to be wise in trying arguably undermined the containment policy and in the end facilitated the fall of

South Vietnam (as well as Laos and Cambodia). The political fallout at home from the war vitiated the realpolitik instincts of the Democratic party and eroded basic confidence in the integrity and good judgment of the U.S. government in the hearts and minds of at least two generations of young Americans.

Covert operations are hard to control. To continue with the Vietnam case, getting rid of Diem was not supposed to eliminate him physically, but it did. It wasn't supposed to, but Operation Prometheus, a NATO crisis contingency plan, served as the unwitting vehicle for junior officers to seize control of the Greek government in April 1967.

Beware the seductive attraction of sanctions.

The general ineffectiveness of sanctions notwithstanding — as detailed above — they still appeal for two main reasons. Firstly, a uniquely American bias exists — which no amount of contrary evidence seems to be able to dispel — that given sufficient economic incentive, or faced with sufficient economic pain, a government can be induced to do or not to do just about anything. This is just not true.

Secondly, sanctions appear to be a middle course, more than just talk, but not as dangerous or as costly as sending troops. When outraged by a Friendly Tyrant's conduct, they show displeasure without much risk or pain. They show the Congress that an administration is "doing something"; or the electorate that Congress is "doing something." Sanctions imposed to pacify domestic audiences, however, may not have the same affect abroad, and usually they do not.

The demand for sanctions in the United States usually confuses activism with narcissism. Activism alters the situation. Narcissism merely makes the invoker feel good — hardly a suitable foreign policy goal. The moral strand of U.S. foreign policy thinking shows no more vividly than in the often fruitless and desultory debates over the utility of sanctions. It is as if, among those who habitually favor sanctions as sending "a moral signal," the mere articulation of American umbrage is going to bring a country to its knees in contrition. Well, it doesn't.

Sanctions against Rhodesia in 1966 — the refusal to import Rhodesian chrome and the Byrd amendment — represent a classic example of counterproductive and self-indulgent sanctions.

Do not depend on multilateral organizations, but do not ignore their utility either.

Multilateral organizations are diplomatic shadows cast by their member states. And, as the British scholar Charles A.W. Manning once wrote, "you do not affect the position of a shadow by doing things to the shadow."

The Organization of American States (OAS) and the United Nations (U.N.) have a mixed history. These organizations worked well in the early postwar period because their deliberations were dominated by the West (in the U.N.) or by the United States (in the OAS). But they have not worked effectively more recently; indeed, the more a conflict was discussed in their chambers, the less the chance of a resolution; conversely, removing an issue from the international agenda signalled that serious diplomacy was about to begin. In the last few years, a partial convergence of U.S. and Soviet interests in settling regional conflicts has made the U.N. more useful. Certainly it proved useful in managing the Kuwait crisis. But it works only when strong countries want it to work, and no one should imagine that the U.N. acted with independent authority after August 2, 1990, in a way that it did not before.

Views expressed by multilateral organizations should never be allowed to drive or heavily circumscribe U.S. policy, however. They did for a time in 1978, when the Carter administration allowed weak and self-interested actors like Venezuela and Mexico to frame the parameters of U.S. policy in Nicaragua, and the result was melancholic.

Still, multilateralism can bestow added legitimacy to U.S. policies, and this is particularly useful in Latin America. Had the OAS been cultivated in advance of the U.S. government's Panama invasion of December 1989, it might have helped reduce the political damage of this example of "Yanqui imperialism."

Say what you will in private to a Friendly Tyrant, and go public only when private avenues have been exhausted.

If the U.S. government has something important to tell a Friendly Tyrant, the message will get through just as well in private.

To be sure, little political satisfaction is derived from a private as opposed to a public venting of views, but skillful statecraft requires such sacrifices. Dressing down a tyrant in public makes for drama on the evening news, at times it may be useful in bolstering the morale of a democratic opposition, and it may even win votes in the next election, but it often has a counterproductive effect in the target country. In the effort to be done with a tyrant, it is critical not to allow him to wrap himself in the flag and pose as a defender of national honor against the Americans. Private communication deprives the tyrant of that ammunition.

For example, U.S. entreaties and pressures on Papa Doc Duvalier in Haiti in the early 1960s enabled Duvalier to manipulate the racial pride and antagonism that lay at the center of Haitian nationalism. U.S. pressures brought to bear against Pinochet in Chile during the Carter administration strengthened him with his core constituencies, as did public American statements about Marcos and Noriega.

American pressures short of using force helped Manuel Noriega stay in power in Panama. Particularly in a country that was virtually created by the U.S. government and dominated by it (to the point that dollars are the currency), sensitivity to U.S. interventionism is acute. Many Panamanians who harbored no affection or admiration for Noriega rallied to his support when the level of U.S. involvement (e.g., the U.S.-supported coup attempt of March 1988) rose to what was for them a humiliating level. In the end, the U.S. military held the highest trump, but until we used it, U.S. rhetoric helped Noriega more than it hurt him.

Plot a falling tyrant's exodus with care, deciding where an ousted dictator should go into exile exclusively on the basis of U.S. interests.
The dictator's attitude to giving up and going into exile is likely to be defined by several considerations: How much loyalty do I command? If I leave, will my family and I be physically safe? Will I be able to bring enough of my fortune with me to live comfortably? Will I be able to depart in relative honor, giving the appearance of having agreed to a transition government? Will I be able to protect my associates who remain behind? Will I retain any influence in the country?

Some tyrants — Trujillo, François Duvalier, Somoza, Noriega — positively enjoy tweaking the U.S. government's nose, and are determined all the more to stay because Washington publicly says they should go. Temperament and circumstance explain why Jean-Claude Duvalier acceded and Noriega developed a bunker mentality. Baby Doc used his inherited power to acquire money, and once he accumulated a satisfactory amount, he lost interest in Haitian politics. He did not try to make any deals or to to protect his associates, and he unabashedly kept a U.S. aircraft idling on the runway while he and his family enjoyed one last champaign bash in the presidential palace.

It may seem like a trivial matter where the dictator goes once he decides to give up power (a problem known sometimes as taking out the trash), but it is not. When a deposed dictator makes his exile in the United States, it may well influence the politics of the country he left behind.

This is not a new dilemma, either — it didn't start with the shah or Ferdinand Marcos. The first major Friendly Tyrants episode of the postwar period involved a similar question. When Fulgenio Batista left Cuba on the last day of 1958, he went into exile in the Dominican

Republic. But Rafael Trujillo began to extort money from Batista to allow him to stay there. As a result, Batista petitioned the U.S. government to let him into the United States, prompting long and careful deliberations by the State Department. In the end, it refused to admit Batista, and found him an exile in Franco's Spain (yet another service to U.S. interests provided by a Friendly Tyrant).

But things were not always handled so well. The Eisenhower administration supported the hated Venezuelan dictator Marcos Pérez Jiménez for years, then offered asylum to him and his chief of police after their overthrow in 1958. Accordingly, when Vice-President Richard Nixon visited Latin America on behalf of President Eisenhower in 1959, he was treated rudely almost everywhere he went, but he was almost killed in Caracas. Nixon was clearly the unfortunate recipient of Venezuelan popular opinion on Pérez Jiménez's choice of exile.

The shah's flight to the United States may not have caused the seizure of the U.S. embassy in Tehran, but it provided the perfect pretext. Ferdinand Marcos tried to stage a comeback from U.S. soil, and his security police engaged in violent acts on U.S. soil both before and after his exile. Alfredo Stroessner asked permission to come to the United States after he was deposed in February 1989, but there was good reason not to let him in, and his request was denied. America's image in Paraguay should be keyed to the chances for democracy, not the chances for the restoration of a dictatorship. Stroessner lives comfortably in Brazil.

Sometimes it is important to arrange a suitable place of exile in advance. Convincing the shah to leave Iran was facilitated by Anwar Sadat's courageous offer to him of refuge. Extracting Jean-Claude Duvalier from Haiti was made easier by the promise of exile in France. If the United States had not indicted Noriega, thereby locking him into Panama on account of extradition treaties, he might have accepted Spain's offer of exile. These little things matter a great deal in the dying moments of a regime.

8   Coordinate Policy

> *We must all hang together, or assuredly we shall all hang separately.*
>
> — Benjamin Franklin

Effective policy requires coordination within the U.S. government. For the Congress, lobbying groups, prestige media, and others to play a constructive role, the executive branch must win their cooperation. The more a Friendly Tyrants problem becomes headline news, the less control over policy the executive branch will retain; therefore, head off the emergence of dictatorial media celebrities.

Honesty really is the best policy.

Lies rarely work. Try to manipulate the press, and it will turn on you. The press is not the only target of manipulation, but different branches of government try to mislead each other, and sometimes the American people as a whole. But in the United States, the truth usually comes out, and it usually comes out sooner rather than later. When public servants lie, it almost always comes back to haunt them — and an unpleasant truth is all the more uncomfortable when preceded by a failed lie.

What's more, the higher the status of the liar, the more trouble a lie causes. Democratic governments are not in the business of either tricking their people or protecting them from the truth. Baron Sonnino, the Italian Foreign Minister during World War I, had a Latin aphorism carved over the mantelpiece of his study: "Aliis licet; tibi non licet" or, "Others may, you may not." Just so.

Documents show that the Johnson administration provided a much rosier picture of the progress being made in South Vietnam to the American people than administration principals themselves believed. The credibility gap, as it was called, cast a shadow over everything else the administration said. The press, which had been friendly toward the administration after the 1964 election, became bitterly hostile by 1968.

The secret bombing of Cambodia by the Nixon administration in early 1969 soon became known to all on May 9, 1969. Richard Nixon was forced out of office for his attempted cover-up of Watergate; but had it not been for the early spate of lying and deception, the press and the rest of the country might not have been so untrusting and suspicious from the outset of Watergate.

President Reagan did not get far when he denied that the U.S. government sought to trade arms to Iran for hostages. Secretary of State James Baker should not have lied in 1990 about U.S. contacts with the Chinese leadership after the massacre in Tiananmen Square. There is just no such thing as a "white lie" when it is the president of the United States or members of his cabinet who are speaking.

Don't let foreign policy issues be captured by the wrong parts of the government.

The way a Friendly Tyrants case first gets defined influences how it develops. The National Center for Disease Control is not the Department of Defense or State, and it has no business running foreign policy. But it will if you let it.

The Haiti crisis of 1986 first arose as a result of domestic concerns: boat people from Haiti landing in Florida brought with them AIDS and a new opportunity to raise questions about inequities in U.S. immigration laws. As a result, certain bureaucracies — like the Immigration and Naturalization Service, Health and Human Services, and the National Center for Disease Control — were tasked with managing the Haitian issue, and not others, like the State and Defense Departments. As the crisis became more intense, the U.S. government took quite a while to shift gears.

Another example concerns Greece. Because of the juxtaposition of the Truman Doctrine and the Greek civil war, the CIA always had a larger than usual role in U.S.-Greek relations as they developed in the 1950s and 1960s. But the CIA is not set up to run the lion's share of an important bilateral relationship. Had authority in the U.S. government for Greek affairs been rechannneled — normalized, as it were — in the 1950s and early 1960s, U.S. reactions to the April 1967 coup might have been more normal, too.

Beware the trap of multiple audiences.

When a politician speaks, he addresses many audiences at once. Efforts to rally the home front can communicate unintended signals abroad, while sending a message abroad can raise tempests domestically.

Americans sometimes misunderstand or misuse a message intended for foreign audiences. When the Reagan administration came into office in January 1981, it sought to translate its campaign rhetoric into policy and signal to adversaries that the Reagan revolution meant no more business as usual. Toward this end, the State Department produced a White Paper on the Marxist-Leninist insurgency in El Salvador, blamed Nicaragua, Cuba, and the Soviet Union for the trouble, and Secretary of State Alexander M. Haig vowed to go to the source of the problem if need be. The White Paper and attendant rhetoric where clearly designed to convey a message to foreign adversaries.

But the domestic opposition — Democrats, the Left, human rights lobbies — listened closely and declared that "another Vietnam" was on the way. Specifically, they recalled the White Papers on Vietnam of 1963-64. Opposition to the Reagan administration's policies was galvanized faster than otherwise would have been the case. Thus, when the administration tried to overturn the restrictions of the Humphrey-Kennedy amendment when it came to Argentina, the opposition to it was already organized and in place, and defeated the effort.

The multiple audience problem also explains in part why it is so hard to reward movement in a positive direction by a tyrant who is disliked in the United States, for there will always be those claiming that it is not enough. By most objective measures, first the Diem regime, and later the Thieu regime, made important strides toward a more decent and effective government in South Vietnam, despite the pressures of war. But it was never enough to satisfy important and powerful domestic constituencies in the United States.

At other times, foreigners misunderstand a domestic message. In 1984, the Reagan administration sought to sell arms, including advanced aircraft, to Jordan. To blunt Jewish (and therefore Congressional) opposition to the sale, the president himself addressed the American Jewish Congress to lobby for his plan. This made sense in terms of domestic politics, but it made a terrible impression in Jordan and throughout the Middle East. The sight of the president of the United States pleading with the Jewish lobby to let the U.S. government pursue the sale humiliated King Hussein.

Finally, we come again to Panama. The preemptive ruling out of the use of force was meant to satisfy Congressional opinion and calm public nerves. Indeed, Congressional approval of the administration's plan for the invocation of sanctions was purchased by the pledge not to use force. Again, concern about a domestic audience sent the wrong signal to a foreign one.

Do not ignore or abuse Congress.

No administration can afford to ignore Congress. The executive branch must draw upon Congress not only because it can be useful, but because antagonizing it with neglect can lead it to plot obstructions. If Congress cannot trust the president, it will be tempted to oppose him.

President Nixon bombed Cambodia and Laos in secret and, for his trouble, got the War Powers Act in return. Even the Tonkin Gulf resolution of 1964 was in a way an abuse of Congress, for Congress was not told of the events preceding the incidents in the Tonkin Gulf that, quite clearly, precipitated the North Vietnamese attack. When Congress rescinded the resolution years later, the psychological impact was considerable.

President Reagan's administration tried to set up a Jordanian rapid deployment force without Congressional knowledge or approval. The idea was not bad; hiding the entire thing from Congress was. When the notion was found out by Congress, it was leaked to foil the plan, with the additional result of embarrassing King Hussein and harming U.S.-Jordanian relations.

And President Bush's decision to propitiate the Chinese government after Tiananmen Square behind Congress's back prompted Congress to oppose him on the question of Chinese students' visas to stay in the United States. In physics, we know, energy is conserved, every action bringing forth an equal and opposite reaction. In politics, the tendency is for ego and honor to be conserved, a much messier process.

Discourage Congress from passing legislation or taking other initiatives to pressure Friendly Tyrants . . .

It's a nice impulse for Congress to want to help out the national interest by doing the things it knows how to do — passing laws. But it is not feasible. Legislation is too inflexible a tool to contend with the subtle and fast-moving problems raised by Friendly Tyrants. Laws intended to cure one set of problems can create others. The propensity of Congress to micromanage the executive function in foreign policy weakens American leadership because it confuses our friends and our adversaries alike. When Congressional intrusion ends up embedded in law, an already difficult relationship is usually made worse. In the final analysis, diplomats and politicians have to rely on their best judgments, and cannot work effectively if beset by regulations. Bad legislation, or legislation that outlives its usefulness, is like a nail without a head: easy to knock in, very hard to get out.

Article I, paragraph 2 of the Mutual Defense Assistance between Cuba and the United States of March 7, 1952, stipulated that the arms flow would cease if American arms were used by a foreign government against its own people. The U.S. arms supply relationship with Cuba, as well as with other Latin American governments at the time, stipulated the use of weapons only for "hemispheric defense" unless Washington gave specific consent for other uses. The unhappy effect of this law, as used against Batista in March 1958, can still be seen in Havana today, in the person of Fidel Castro.

Congress really inserted itself in the foreign policy decision process in 1974, when it passed the War Powers Act and the Budget Reform Act. Both these laws restrict executive branch power. The War Powers Act enables Congress to cut off funding after sixty days for any American military deployment overseas not covered by a formal declaration of war. The Budget Reform Act provides Congress with more opportunities to intervene in the policy process, enabling congressmen to hone in more efficiently on particular programs.

The Humphrey-Kennedy amendment of 1976, ending the supply of U.S. military equipment to Argentina and Chile, weakened neither dictatorship. It did exact an economic price, however, as American firms lost access to the markets and military establishments of these two countries. It also rendered the United States an undependable supplier, costing it arms business elsewhere in the Third World.

The Clark amendment of 1975 banned the United States from intervening in any respect into the Angolan civil war for fear that intervention would produce "another Vietnam," another commitment to an undeserving Friendly Tyrant. The amendment instead cleared the way for a more intensive Soviet-Cuban intervention, the birth of an unfriendly tyrant, and eventually a base for tens of thousands of Cuban troops in southern Africa.

Congress has made great use of its powers of the purse. At last count, more than five hundred statutory amendments to the Foreign Aid Bill have accumulated over the years, very few of which have to do with money or aid as such. Even obscure amendments to the Foreign Assistance Act often hinder U.S. diplomacy. Take amendment 513 of the Foreign Assistance Act, passed by Congress in 1986, which suspends American aid to autocratic governments that come to power by overthrowing democratically elected leaders. It sounds good in theory, but what happens if the democrats are anti-American and the autocrats are pro-American? This is what happened when the Sudanese government of Sadiq al-Mahdi was overthrown on June 30, 1989, by a military coup.

Mahdi had been close to Libya, but the new leaders professed themselves pro-Egyptian and so, by association, pro-Western. But thanks to amendment 513, Washington was obligated to suspend its assistance to the Sudanese government. A presidential waiver was required to override the law.

Another example was the Smith amendment of 1985 which prevented all foreign military sales to Jordan "unless the President has certified to the Congress that Jordan is publicly committed to the recognition of Israel and to prompt entry into peace negotiations with Israel." Again in March 1991, Congress voted to deny Jordan $55 million in aid against administration urging unless it demonstrated a commitment to an open peace process. While these Congressional measures were well intentioned, Jordan is more likely to do such helpful things if it can protect itself from predatory neighbors, like Syria or Iraq, and feed its population, than if it cannot. Not every proposed U.S. military sale to Jordan can be justified on this basis, but some can. Laws like the Smith amendment make it impossible to see and act on such distinctions.

The Cyprus Report, too, has been a source of tension. After the Greek junta overthrew Archbishop Makarios and troops from the Republic of Turkey were dispatched to part of that island in 1974, Congress mandated a twice yearly report on the status of Cyprus and the efforts aimed at settling its conflict. Each time this report appears, at least one of the disputing parties is angered, and sometimes all of them, quite needlessly. As a result, the report works against conciliation. The trouble goes on year after year because there is not enough of a consensus to remove this piece of legislation from the books, proving that bad legislation is much harder to remove than to enact.

The Non-Proliferation Act of 1978 requires the President to certify whether or not certain countries possess nuclear weapons, and if they do, U.S. aid programs are automatically suspended. In recent years, this certification process has most pointedly involved Pakistan, which clearly has an advanced nuclear program and probably has all the components to make a fission weapon. But Zia was a Friendly Tyrant of special significance, given his role in the effort to block Soviet control of Afghanistan. Both the Carter and Reagan administrations saw Pakistani cooperation in Afghanistan as more urgent than concerns about nuclear proliferation. To declare in the 1980s that Pakistan lacked nuclear weapons was like saying that a person carrying a gun, but not having yet put bullets in the chamber, is unarmed. Nevertheless, each year, the Pakistani certification charade was carried out.

Congressional intrusion into the executive prerogative in foreign policy has led to a dialectic of contention and evasion which, while not unique in American history, corrodes coherent policy making more than ever before. Thus, the series of Boland amendments, restricting executive branch efforts to fund the Contras, led key Reagan administration figures to break the law. In turn, such acts by the executive encouraged the Congress further to extend its intrusive oversight. Indeed, each branch sees the other, at least from time to time, as having tyrannical aspirations to dictate policy.

. . . But if Congress does intrude, try to make the best of it by using it.
Not all legal approaches are bad ideas. Some, at least, have mixed effects. In accordance with Sections 116(d) and 502B (b) of the Foreign Assistance Act, the Department of State has been obligated since 1978 to produce an annual report on human rights situations in countries around the globe. These reports lately exceed thirteen hundred single spaced pages; every page contains a potential irritant to U.S. relations with Friendly Tyrants, and sometimes the potential is realized. But since the report is universal, it singles out no special violator or class of violators. The very existence of the report may encourage recipients of U.S. foreign aid to clean up their acts. But whether such effects really exist, and whether, if they do, they outweigh the problems caused, remains unclear.

With proper coordination, Congressional stipulations can allow the U.S. government to play a good cop-bad cop game with tyrants. The Mica amendment of 1981, for example, specified certain human rights standards before U.S. aid could be disbursed. Congress had Haiti in mind at the time, and the amendment did work to increase the leverage of U.S. diplomats on Jean-Claude Duvalier's government, with some positive results.

This said, most legislative initiatives have negative effects. Even if it is helpful at times for a diplomat to be able to say "my hands are tied," diplomats do not often want their hands to be tied. If you don't believe it, find some experienced U.S. diplomats and ask them.

Learn the proper care and feeding of the press, for even a hostile journalist has business interests.
Until quite recently, practically all postwar U.S. presidents, particularly the Republican ones, have complained about unfair treatment from the press. Even today, the motives of politicians are regularly impugned, their staffs hounded, and their performance held to impossible standards.

Most of them would surely agree with the playwright Tom Stoppard's characterization of the press as a stalking horse masquerading as a sacred cow.

But the press is not an implacable enemy. The journalist, whatever his political views, is a professional and a businessman. The government official has something the journalist wants — information — and so he has some leverage. Provide honest and useful information, and the press is likely to offer respectful treatment, if not adulation, in return. As a result, officials should have faith that truthful and sensible views will be aired if they are repeated often enough and explained with full candor.

Most of the press was skeptical in 1981 that the Salvadoran government of José Napoleon Duarte was reform-minded. They believed instead that only U.S. pressures brought to bear against him could make a positive difference. The Reagan administration persisted in its arguments that support would work better than pressure and, in time, most journalistic doubters had to admit that this was so.

Remind the Friendly Tyrant you would preserve that "out of sight is out of mind."

When the topic is Friendly Tyrants, the distance between *The Washington Post* and *The National Enquirer* is not always that great; both were fascinated by Imelda Marcos's wardrobe and Jean-Claude Duvalier's collection of lewd magazines. When the press gets a hold of a spectacular tale of vulgarity, greed, cruelty, and avarice in a foreign ally of the United States, the story can take on a life of its own.

For this reason, Friendly Tyrants are better off not talking to the American press, and there may even be rare occasions when U.S. officials might proffer such advice. Alfredo Stroessner almost never gave interviews, so he had virtually no persona in the United States. Neither does Indonesia's Suharto. Contrast this with a loudmouth dictator like Marcos or Noriega, and the difference becomes obvious.

Avoiding being stunned by nomad journalists is just as important. Major American newspapers occasionally send a star correspondent (like *New York Times* reporter Barbara Crossette) on a regional tour, and the product is a series of long feature articles that run for several days in a row. The appearance of such reporters in the capital of a long neglected country becomes a major local event, bringing people and information out of the woodwork. The stories that subsequently appear often have much new information and cause a stir both in the country and in the United States, often with unpredictable effects. When a major newspaper offers five articles in as many days on, say, Suharto and Indonesia, it may amount to twice the total column space devoted to those topics in the previous year or two. Anyone interested in Indonesia in the government, the press, the lobbies, the Congress, is going to be galvanized into action by such exposure.

Star reporters are less attracted to capital cities when they cannot interview senior figures. Nomad journalists regularly visited the Philippines in the years before Marcos's fall, but no one went to Paraguay in the years before Stroessner's collapse, which is one reason why it took so many years for him to do so.

Do not indulge in post hoc acrimony when a Friendly Tyrants crisis goes awry, for this hinders future effectiveness.

Ideally, policy ought to be coordinated not just across U.S. government agencies at any given time, but between administrations, as well — through time, as it were. This is extraordinarily difficult to do, of course, but since Democratic and Republican administrations more or less alternate every so many years, it makes sense for both — and certainly it makes sense for the country — to be reserved in their criticism of the foreign policy errors or misfortunes of others. Polemics lead to exaggerations, and in a country where foreign policy is the business of so many people, past crises that went awry are politicized and distorted. People get carried away: with so much partisan vituperation in the air, it is often hard to distinguish between the polemic and the truth, sometimes even for those who invent the polemic.

Unhealthy acrimony over Friendly Tyrants episodes has been with us for a long time. Debate over Vietnam, in particular, helped destroy the bipartisan consensus on foreign policy that had existed since the early 1940s. Democrats blamed Republicans, political appointees blamed bureaucrats, the Department of State blamed the Department of Defense, civilians in the Office of the Secretary of Defense blamed military brass, politicians blamed the press, youth blamed their seniors — and all vice-versa too — and nothing has been the same since. Vietnam tore the country apart, and did deep damage to American foreign policy.

Failures in Iran and Nicaragua cast long shadows, too. It simply is not true that the Carter administration deliberately undermined the shah or sought a Sandinista victory in Nicaragua. On the other hand, it is also not true that everything was fine in Nicaragua until the Reagan administration's policies forced Managua into the arms of Havana and Moscow.

This acrimony probably cannot be prevented, but experts ought at least (as Dick Gregory once put it) establish the truth before they tamper with it. And basic respect for those who erred must always be maintained. A big difference exists between a mistake and a crime, between subsequent disagreement over historical interpretation and accusations about who "disgraced the flag." We do ourselves no service when we lose sight of these distinctions.

9 Hedge Bets

Bud Abbott: "Hey Lou, what took you so long?"
Lou Costello: "I took a short cut."

Assume a gap between expectations and the actual power of U.S. policy to influence outcomes. Hedge bets by planning a healthy margin for error into every strategy.

Do not assume the United States is central to a Friendly Tyrants crisis outcome.

Americans have often seen their own actions as critical, perhaps more so than was the case.

When China fell to the communists in 1948-49, an assumption underlying the acrimonious ensuing debate in the United States was that American policy caused the fiasco and, by implication, could have prevented it. Not so: it was not in American hands to buy Mao Tse-tung or arm Chiang Kai-shek in such a way as to change the outcome. The fall of the shah and the rise of Khomeini prompted a similar debate, one which simply assumed U.S. foreign policy was the most central variable. Granted, the U.S. government was important. But so were developments in Iranian society during the shah's reign over which the U.S. government had little control — urbanization, increased social mobility, the marginalization of the clergy's political power, the development of mass media, and so forth.

The Vietnam War induced a new sensitivity to what the U.S. government cannot do. This was a natural reaction to a disaster born of hubris. If not carried too far, it is a healthy development.

But the tendency seems to be again to overstate the U.S. role. Take the events of early 1986. Flush with success in the Haitian and Philippine crises, some officials were emboldened to see General Noriega as a piece of cake. He wasn't.

Journalists are even more prone to overestimate American power. As an example of this, note what an American reporter who spent time in Burma during the upheavals of 1988 concluded: "the smallest gesture of U.S. military support — perhaps nothing more than a couple of battleships off the Burmese coast and a few warplanes in it skies — could have won the day for the Burmese people."[1] But if it's as easy as that, why do such tactics never seem to work?

Remember that — short of a U.S. invasion — local forces decide political struggles.

The trick for American policy makers most of the time is to bring to bear enough of a U.S. presence to move developments in the right direction, but not so much as to commit the U.S. government to direct involvement. Indeed, knowing a country well means knowing what U.S. policy can achieve by indirection.

Going back to the 1950s, getting rid of Trujillo and failing to get rid of Papa Doc are both fine examples of mismanagement. In the former case, Washington did not realize the extent of Trujillo's thuggery, which was more than enough to foil the Kennedy administration's transition plan. As for Papa Doc Duvalier's regime, which moved into the spotlight shortly thereafter: he was a more popular president, the Tonton Macoute a more formidable force, and the opposition to his rule less serious than was thought. So an artificial military crisis launched from the Dominican Republic in 1962 and a clumsily attempted coup both failed to oust Duvalier.

Even successes, if carefully analyzed after the fact, bear out this point. While U.S. policy in the Philippine case was masterful, "people power" in the end was the single most important factor. U.S. diplomats were not the ones who stood their ground against tanks and machine guns bearing down upon them. Jean-Claude Duvalier's exit from Haiti in 1986 was only partly a result of U.S. policy; had it not been for Radio Soleil and the mobilization undertaken by the Catholic church, Duvalier might be yet ruling in Port-au-Prince.

The Panamanian fiasco of 1988-89 was a textbook case of getting it wrong, until an invasion by American troops settled the matter, at least temporarily. In Washington in 1987 it was believed that General Noriega was isolated and ripe for a fall, so sanctions were imposed. The Civic Crusade appeared to be a legitimate mass movement for a time, and Noriega's patronage network in the military and civil service seemed weak. But then, relying precisely on these bases, Noriega crushed the Civic Crusade and the two coup attempts that followed.

As these examples suggest, Washington tends most often to overestimate its strength in the small countries of Central America.

High profile activities by the U.S. government in themselves disturb local dynamics — a sort of political Heisenberg effect — but without endowing the U.S. government with concomitant control over them. Working by indirection thus cuts two ways; failure isn't free. When you begin messing around in a country, as in the Dominican Republic in 1961, well, you sometimes make a mess.

Do not assume that the sheer size of the United States guarantees success . . .

The belief that U.S. power is too great to fail encourages policy makers to begin courses of action whose end they have not fully thought through. It makes more sense to plan on the basis of worst-case scenarios. Better to overestimate what it takes than to underestimate, for almost every problem takes longer, costs more, and generates more internal opposition than initially appears to be the case.   Avoid open-ended commitments; ignore those peddling easy solutions. Or, metaphorically: It is better to remain childless than to father an orphan.

The U.S. commitment to South Vietnam was the quintessential case of hubris and open-ended commitment. No decision was ever taken to go to war in Vietnam; rather, a series of small escalations built up the American stake. The U.S. government simply assumed that a small and poor country like North Vietnam could not defeat the United States. In 1964, in 1965, and again in 1967 the Department of Defense established self-imposed limits on the level of fighting; it blithely assumed that U.S. goals could be achieved with a limited and definable level of effort.[2] This led to what amounted to an open-ended commitment that, in the end, violated the Pentagon's self-imposed limits many times over without bringing victory. Had the U.S. government taken the challenge more seriously, it would probably have made a more generous estimate of what was required for victory.

One would have thought that the lesson of Vietnam would have been enough of a base to learn from, but it was not. The Carter administration's policy toward Nicaragua under Somoza operated on the assumption that nothing taking place in Nicaragua could seriously endanger U.S. security. With this in mind, the responsibility for policy was vouchsafed in the State Department's Bureau on Humanitarian Affairs! As the likelihood of a Sandinista takeover grew, those with a more strategic view claimed control of the policy process, but even then, the use of force to prevent a Sandinista victory was never seriously considered. The State Department seemed to believe that the Sandinistas could be prevented from pursuing an anti-U.S. regional policy through the sheer weight of American power.

In Panama, the Reagan administration took an alarmingly casual view about how to get rid of Manuel Noriega. It looked so easy in a country dominated by the American economy, hosting vast numbers of American soldiers. Further, most of the Panamanian people were positively disposed toward the United States, while the dictator was mildly unpopular and lacked allies. Mistaken assumptions of a rollover led to one mistake after another. Some research would have prevented most of them. An expert on Panama would have explained that Noriega's constituency was wider than supposed and his personality tougher; that blanket sanctions would be counterproductive; and that failure to oust Noriega quickly would embolden him to make common cause with the Sandinistas, the Cubans, and the Soviets. But because Noriega seemed to be such an easy mark, serious study of the situation was deemed unnecessary in many important quarters.

... But remember that the U.S. government is usually perceived as more powerful than it is.

However, Washington's new-found relative modesty is not shared by the rest of the world, most of which still overestimates the role of the U.S. government. Now that Soviet power has fallen so suddenly on such hard times, the exaggeration of U.S. influence has grown even further. Many foreign leaders are prone to scapegoating their own failures, often by taking recourse in conspiracy theory. To take a classic example, Gamal Abdul Nasser accused the U.S. government of having fought for Israel in the 1967 war, for in no other way could he account to his people for Egypt's military loss. Oppositions, including the weak and divided one in Haiti during the Duvalier period, blamed Washington for propping up the tyrant when in fact their own lack of support or skill better explained their political impotence.

This attitude implies that the U.S. government is often perceived as more powerful than is the case. If extreme care is exercised, that perception can possibly be exploited by American officials.

Do not engage the office or person of the president in a Friendly Tyrants episode unless a favorable outcome is certain.

Friendly Tyrants do not begin as first-order policy problems. Accordingly, they tend to be handled at the working level. Then the choice arises whether to engage the person and status of the president in such matters. Given the doleful American record, it appears preferable to keep the president clear and protected from the possibility of failure. He should act the role of the coach, directing the action behind the scenes. If the policy succeeds, there are always ways of taking credit; if it fails, the assistants will take the fall. The American president who goes hunting for Friendly Tyrants risks ending up as the prey.

Presidents often ignore this advice and insert themselves in Friendly Tyrants episodes, ending up with tarnished reputations. Jimmy Carter said more than he needed to in both the Nicaraguan and Iranian crises of 1978-79. He thereby hitched his political fortunes to the outcomes of those crises, with unhappy consequences for his 1980 presidential campaign. George Bush called for Noriega's removal when the latter stole and bloodied the Panamanian election of May 1989. The president of the United States had to eat his words, however, at least until Noriega provided the pretext for Washington to be done with him.

If you resort to force to either preserve or topple a Friendly Tyrant, make sure that force is decisive.

The biggest mistake the United States has made in the postwar period, arguably, was applying force to save South Vietnam and failing to save it. It is not necessarily the case that using more force would have won the conflict; in retrospect, "how?" to use force seems to have been the proper question in the Vietnam case, not "how much?" force to use. The scale of U.S. efforts was not what mattered, but their wisdom. Certainly, using force decisively depends on more than massive strength and firepower; it depends on intelligent application.

Nevertheless, overwhelming force can help in many instances. The December 1989 U.S. invasion of Panama left no doubt from the start as to who was going to win. This clarity probably affected casualty figures — making them lower on all sides — and shortened the core crisis period. The decisive use of force shortens its use, and that makes it politically more manageable. Certainly, on those very rare occasions when a president decides that force is the only way, squeamish public opinion must not deter him. In such circumstances, it is generally better to ask forgiveness than permission.

Notes

1 Stan Sesser, "Are Invasions Sometimes O.K.?" *The New York Times*, January 17, 1990.
2 See Richard Betts and Leslie Gelb, *The Irony of Vietnam: The System Worked* (Washington, D.C.: Brookings, 1982).

10 Plan for Crises

> *We wish experience to make us not shrewder for*
> *next time, but wise forever.*
> — Jacob Burckhardt

Do not try to predict crises but do plan for them. Be ready for questions about what has happened, and prepare options for U.S. policy.

Assume that a crisis will occur tomorrow morning, but don't cry wolf.
Being responsible for a country often leads bureaucrats to become convinced that their client is the key to U.S. national security; usually it is not. Appreciating this impulse of bureaucrats to live life on a heroic scale, decision makers generally discount their appeals to vigilance.

The line between a difficult impasse and a real crisis is not always clear, but top decision makers can tell the difference in symptoms: a crisis is when they spend large amounts of time thinking, meeting, and making decisions about a single issue. The crisis is over when they spend time in more usual ways.

The secret of any successful business is proper planning. In order not to be ignored, experts should hold their peace until asked for analysis and advice. When asked, they must be ready with answers. Like soldiers, they must be painstaking and calm, but ever ready. Unfortunately, the State Department building is not as conducive to patience as a bunker.

Contingency plans are sometimes worth very little, for reality invariably imposes unexpected dimensions. Plans developed in 1949 envisioned the withdrawal of American troops from the Korean peninsula; there were no plans drawn up for fighting a three-year war there. But when the North Korean invasion came in June 1950, that is just what we did, plans or no plans. But the planning process, as distinct from the plans themselves, is important not only because it just might correspond to the crises that actually occur. Even if it does not, planning has the effect of raising possibilities and questions to be thought through, so that the government's potential to be nimble at the crucial time is enlarged. It is as impossible to predict crises as it is to predict where lightning will strike, but planning can and must go forward anyway.

Failure to plan leads to very embarrassing results. No one expected a major crisis in Iran in January 1978, and that was entirely excusable. But still to have no plans in May 1978 was inexcusable. No one knew when Major Moisés Giroldi would get it into his head to try to oust General Noriega in Panama, and no one could have known. But not to have had a plan ready in October 1989, five months after President Bush had so loudly inveighed against Noriega, was reason for wonderment.

Having plans that work, on the other hand, is a joy to behold. The United States managed to come up with a specific plan to defend Saudi Arabia and liberate Kuwait after August 2, 1990, because it had thought about defending that area for more than a decade, and trained for it. Critics who said American efforts would not work in a desert when planning had been geared to Europe underestimated or misunderstood American military planning in the 1980s.

Head off the emergence of tyrannical celebrities if you can, or any ensuing crisis will defy professional management.

Once dictatorial celebrities emerge, a Friendly Tyrants case is virtually out of professional control. Once Baby Doc Duvalier's champagne bashes and pornographic magazines, Imelda Marcos's shoes and New York City real estate, and Manuel Noriega's drugs and election thefts became the stuff of tabloids, American officials lost much of their power to shape policy and outcomes. Celebrities arouse the ire of lobbies, attract Congressional attention, and soon find themselves facing public denunciations and emotion-laden demands for economic sanctions. As sentiments begin to drive the policy process, the chances for a coherent U.S. approach diminish.

But how do you head off these things? Sometimes a word to the wise is sufficient. The United States suggested that Haile Selassie not be seen feeding his dogs in the midst of a famine in Ethiopia in 1973; it wasn't enough to save him, but he did take the hint. Sometimes nothing that can be said or done will work; Rafael Trujillo had an obsession for self-adultion that nothing could deter. He even had village water pumps labelled: "Trujillo alone gives us water to drink." In between, everything from discreet ambassadorial representations to more public, but tactful, expressions of concern, can help. Admittedly, however, it isn't easy.

Make sure allies are included in your plans, and that their views are heard and understood before a crisis occurs.
   Policy toward a Friendly Tyrant occasionally must take other powers into account. U.S. policy toward Paraguay depends in part on Brazilian and Argentinean views. In formulating policy toward Tunisia, Paris must be taken into account; the same goes for the Ivory Coast, Chad, and a number of other African countries. The French also have significant forces in Djibouti, just across from Saudi Arabia, the richest Friendly Tyrant of them all.
   Having to consult and work with Paris, Brasilia, and other capitals obviously complicates matters, as third parties obviously have different interests and, sometimes, different goals. But such cooperation is sometimes necessary and the sooner third party roles are integrated into planning, the better. It helps to review relations with allies and friends periodically to understand how they view potential threats, and what their attitudes toward joint operations might be. Unfortunately, the level of liaison and planning among Western allies for distant contingencies, although not entirely absent, is not what it might be. Perhaps the successful example of multinational planning in the Kuwait crisis will help in the future.

If the U.S. embassy staff is competent, pay close attention to its information and views.
   There is no substitute for being there, on the ground, when a crisis breaks out. For certain kinds of public opinion research in the United States, frequenting bars is the best methodology; mutatis mutandis, the same goes in other countries. Not all ambassadors play a role in times of crisis, but crises do give them a chance to shine — and sometimes they do.
   Frank Carlucci, the U.S. ambassador in Lisbon in 1974, persuaded Washington not to give up on Portugal, as Kissinger and others were inclined to do.[1] William H. Sullivan in Iran concluded early on that the shah would have to abdicate and that the Iranian military would crumble rather than shoot at the Ayatollah Khomeini's supporters.[2] Carlucci was listened to, Sullivan was not.

More generally, intelligence personnel spend too little time in a post, and when abroad, they often spend too little time in the field. Even when this is not a problem, other problems take its place. One is that intelligence personnel abroad have trouble recruiting and using foreign nationals effectively because of the U.S. inability to protect such sources and methods. This boils down to an obvious truth: if you can't keep a secret, people won't tell you any.

Do not be seduced by classified information; the essence of what you need to know is in the newspaper.

In almost all cases, to understand a situation properly, books and the morning newspaper are sufficient. Information about Friendly Tyrants collected by clandestine or other sub rosa means sometimes has distortive effects. In a few cases, confidence in it is so high, the U.S. government gets led into disaster.

False intelligence indicating that Colonel Francisco Camaaño was a Castroite "behind the throne" of a returning Juan Bosch in 1965 seems to have been a major factor in persuading Washington to intervene militarily in the Dominican Republic. That intervention stopped Bosch and Camaaño, whatever their intentions were, but it also undermined democracy in the Dominican Republic and sullied the American reputation in the region.

Further, data is not wisdom. Intelligence alone does not solve problems or provide answers. Policy makers must constantly guide the intelligence agencies by asking the right questions. When they fail to, the results are all too clear. As a White House aide observed after the failed coup attempt in Panama if October 1989: "The intelligence wasn't good, and it wasn't made good use of, but that isn't really the point, is it? There wasn't a clear idea of exactly what we wanted to do in case of a coup, so we didn't ask the right questions. And without the right questions, intelligence doesn't help."[3]

To end an interagency meeting with a call for more intelligence means the issue has not been addressed, for intelligence reports can fill the room with paper and still not tell a leader what he ought to do.

Be doubly wary of information that arrives through unorthodox channels.

The Dominican Republic offers a classic example of information drawn from irregular sources. Intelligence indicating that Trujillo was far weaker than he in fact was arrived at the Kennedy White House from Oleg Cassini, author of the Cholly Knickerbocker political gossip column for

The New York Post and a close friend of Joseph Kennedy, the president's father. Cassini had done public relations work for Trujillo through Trujillo's one-time son-in-law, Porfirio Rubirosa. Rubirosa told Cassini a cascade of lies; these were passed on to Joseph Kennedy and then to the president. Perhaps because he was still smarting from the Bay of Pigs fiasco, Kennedy was unusually inclined to trust this odd intelligence source. The faulty information led him to underestimate Trujillo's strength and, partly as a result, the U.S. government totally mismanaged the transition after Trujillo's assassination in May 1961.[4]

If the ousted tyrant takes refuge in the United States, do not prosecute him.

The beginning of the planning process for the next Friendly Tyrants crisis begins before the last one is fully over. As a case in point: to prosecute a fallen Friendly Tyrant once he leaves his country for exile in the United States, even if it is legally justified, makes it that much more difficult to extract the next crooked dictator if coming to the United States is the only way to get him out of his country.

Leaving off prosecution is sometimes the better part of valor. Charges against the dying Ferdinand Marcos (for racketeering violations, of all things) sent warning signals to other Friendly Tyrants who might some day consider taking refuge in the United States. Prosecuting Manuel Noriega sends similar signals, not least in recent times to Samuel Doe, who proved difficult to extract from Monrovia partly because he feared prosecution in the United States. Given the difficulty of persuading those in the Justice Department to leave obvious malfeasants alone, quiet deals among government agencies are probably the best way to proceed. Prosecutive discretion is a bedrock of U.S. law — it should be exercised.

Do not lose interest once a Friendly Tyrant has left the scene, for another crisis may soon occur.

Do not drop the ball just because the biggest tackler has fallen by the wayside. Although seemingly solved at one level, some crises return at another. Sometimes this can be prevented if high level attention does not wane too quickly. This is because top policy makers can make quick decisions that redirect policy, while deputy assistant secretaries cannot. It's bad enough to be discomfited once by a Friendly Tyrant, but to bring it upon yourself a second time is unforgivable.

High-level policy attention toward Haiti in Washington virtually ended soon after the exit of Jean-Claude Duvalier in February 1986, reverting to lower-ranking officials. Those officials quickly understood the enormous problems facing the new Haitian leaders, starting with the absence of raw materials to reconstitute the Haitian government. Three coups d'état then took place, and much blood was shed, but lower ranking U.S. officials found it impossible to attract high-level attention. Without it, the U.S. government could not respond to a changing environment fast enough to keep pace.

Similarly, after Marcos departed and Corazon Aquino came to power, high-level attention naturally lapsed. No one knew if Aquino could run a government, or if she could clean up the mess Marcos had left behind. The land reform programs did not go well, the government began to show signs of profound incompetence, the war against the New People's Army went badly, and the economy lay nearly comatose. Still, top American decision makers paid hardly any attention to developments in the Philippines. A new crisis seems not far off.

After Pinochet lost the presidential plebiscite he held in October 1988, American officials acted as though he was finished as a major political factor in Chile. In fact, he retained a range of options for foiling elections, manipulating the constitution, and even staging another military coup. It was too soon to let the deal go down there, this despite the fact that everything has turned out well for Chilean democracy thus far, and Patricio Aylwin was inaugurated without incident in March 1990.

After the war for Kuwait was won, many urged Washington to turn full attention to the Arab-Israeli crisis. Very bad idea. In 1983, the United States rushed from Lebanon to the Reagan plan of September 1, 1982 with the result that both policies failed. Slow and steady wins the race. Yogi Berra may have said it, but it is still true: It ain't over 'til it's over.

Yet decision makers cannot always be blamed for their short attention spans. Friendly Tyrants are not usually their highest priority nor, despite the enormous amount of trouble they can cause, should they be. After the Carter administration's initial attempt to oust Somoza from Nicaragua failed, its attention turned elsewhere. By the time administration principals focussed in again on Nicaragua, things were much worse, and unexpectedly so. But what were the issues that had diverted their attention? Aside from the Camp David drama, there was the Iranian revolution and the SALT II Treaty . . . that's all. They messed up in Managua, true, but it would have been easy to forgive them — if either Iran or SALT II worked out properly, that is.

Notes

1   See Carlucci's comments in Hans Binnendijk, ed., *Authoritaran Regimes in Transition* (Washington, D.C.: U.S. Department of State, Foreign Service Institute, 1987), pp. 210-11.
2   William H. Sullivan, *Mission to Iran* (New York: W. W. Norton, 1981).
3   Quoted in *The New York Times*, October 10, 1989.
4   Arturo Espaillat, *Trujillo: The Last Caesar* (Chicago, Ill: Regnery, 1963); and Norman Gall, "How Trujillo Died," *The New Republic*, April 13, 1963.

Appendix A: Maxims and Precepts

Maxims and Precepts

1. Beware Dependence

Limit the extent to which U.S. interests depend on Friendly Tyrants. Within such limits, however, pursue beneficial relationships with Friendly Tyrants.

Therefore,

- Remember: the greater the American dependence on a Friendly Tyrant, the greater the risk to U.S. interests over time;
- The best way to get things done is to do them yourself, even if it's more expensive that way;
- Don't send either too large or too small an arsenal to a Friendly Tyrant; help it to defend its territory but not to commit aggression against foreign enemies;
- Do everything possible to make sure that American aid is not used for domestic repression;
- Avoid the "sunken costs" trap; and
- Since interests often change faster than policy, review bilateral relations at the expert level on a regular basis.

2. Be Nimble

Fundamental U.S. interests are usually tied to good relations with a country, not with a particular individual or regime; therefore, avoid gratuitous gestures of friendship toward today's rulers, and you'll have less gratuitous trouble with tomorrow's.

Therefore,

• Don't let relations with a dictator wax any warmer than needed;
• Do not suffocate a Friendly Tyrant with too many visible American connections;
• Aging Friendly Tyrants are the most dangerous, so American diplomats should watch them closely and keep their overnight bags packed;
• Associate the American government with evolving democratic processes, not with individuals or parties;
• Don't assume that allies must share U.S. ideological precepts to be useful;
• Stay in touch with all political factions in a country, even if a Friendly Tyrant objects;
• Don't assume that American support for an authoritarian regime necessarily makes its opponents anti-American; and
• Don't give up the ship — it's never too late to get on the winning side of a Friendly Tyrants crisis.

3. Promote Democracy

U.S. foreign policy should be biased in favor of democratic allies and toward the promotion of democracy in the lands of Friendly Tyrants. This makes sense not just because it is morally right, but because it is pragmatic abroad (ties with democracies are low risk compared to those with Friendly Tyrants) and at home (Americans more readily accept relations with Friendly Tyrants when these are seen as temporary lesser evils about which the U.S. government is not complacent).

Therefore,

• Favor democracies over autocracies whenever there is a realistic choice;

• Encourage democracy in Friendly Tyrants up to, but not beyond, the point of destabilizing an ally for which no better regime replacement exists;

• Don't use American power against democratically elected or locally legitimate governments;

• Seek good relations with all democratic countries, even those few whose governments are tempestuous or anti-American. . .

• . . .But don't let democracy be the only criterion by which policy is decided;

• Generously support Friendly Tyrants who evolve into democrats. . .

• . . .But use American money intelligently or don't use it at all;

• Use U.S. influence to keep the military in the barracks;

• Celebrate the new democrat. . .

• . . .But be patient with those moving ahead more slowly.

4. Chastise with Care

Keep history in mind when making moral judgments about a Friendly Tyrant. Be gentler with the improving autocrat than with the lapsed democrat. Do not assume either that everyone loves democracy or that even the most authoritarian political culture is trapped forever in cycles of repression and revolt. All government is capable of both retrogression and improvement.

Therefore,

• Do not project American standards and values onto other countries;

• Don't rely on metaphors drawn from the American experience to understand other peoples' problems;

• Don't try to turn every story into a two-sided conflict, because not every conflict has good guys and bad guys — or even better and worse guys — from the American point of view;

• Don't assume that everyone loves democracy. . .

• . . .But never assume a country is doomed to be nondemocratic;

• Hold authoritarian allies to their own standards; the more democratic they say they are, the higher the standard to which you should hold them;

• Support indigenous elements seeking legal remedies and legal reform;

• Push harder for democracy in fair weather than in foul;

• Do not even contemplate dissuading a state from pursuing its vital interests; and

• Do not preach.

5. Define Goals

Establish and prioritize goals. In normal times, the appropriate goal is to build a stable relationship with a country that can outlast any particular regime. In crises, the goal is to preserve U.S. interests. The mere retention or removal of a dictator is not a suitable goal.

Therefore,

• Do not allow policy to become personalized around a dictator;
• Ignore cheering squads within the United States, either for the opposition or for the dictator;
• Don't let stability become an end in itself;
• As the Friendly Tyrant's life cycle advances, decide as early as possible on the basis of U.S. interests if and when to abandon reform and seek to remove a tyrant;
• If you choose reform, effectiveness will depend on leaving a tyrant a clear way to reduce U.S. pressures;
• Do not undermine a Friendly Tyrant unless you are sure the alternative will be better;
• Should you choose removal over reform, do not usurp the opposition by declaring an all-out campaign to oust a Friendly Tyrant;
• Worry more about major countries than minor ones. . .
• . . .But don't underestimate the damage that even a "small" Friendly Tyrants crisis can cause.

6. Know the Country

Whatever you wish to do — seek regime reform or a tyrant's removal — take account of local standards and circumstances. Understand how local politics work, then match instruments of American leverage with apt opportunities.

Therefore,

• Keep in mind how unusual the United States is, and therefore how it must not serve as your template for understanding other countries;
• Do not assume you know the role of the military, the church, or political parties: study instead;
• Invoke sanctions only when confident they will change either the leadership or the policies of the country in question for, otherwise, they will be counterproductive;
• Don't forget that the psychological impact of sanctions in the target country is often more important than their practical consequences;
• For sanctions to work at the symbolic level, they have to make basic sense;
• Real expertise is invaluable, so invest in it, acquire it, and use it;
• Adjust career patterns in the U.S. government to encourage specialization; and
• Promote nongovernmental exchanges.

7. Think It Through

Husband policy assets carefully and do not deprive yourself of leverage, even in apparently easy cases. In other words: attend to details; don't make promises or threats you can't keep; avoid open-ended commitments; say whatever you can in private; show no gratuitous enmity; impose sanctions with great caution.

Therefore,

• Do not offer a Friendly Tyrant unconditional support, or let him think that he has it, or U.S. efforts to influence that political culture will diminish;
• Remind a recalcitrant tyrant that alternative allies exist, or the tyrant's willingness to service U.S. foreign policy needs will wane;
• Do not rule out the use of force or covert operations publicly, preemptively, or at all. . .
• . . .But expect unanticipated consequences when using force or stealth;
• Beware the seductive attraction of sanctions;
• Do not depend on multilateral organizations, but do not ignore their utility either;
• Say what you will in private to a Friendly Tyrant, and go public only when private avenues have been exhausted; and
• Plot a falling tyrant's exodus with care, deciding where an ousted dictator should go into exile exclusively on the basis of U.S. interests.

8. Coordinate Policy

Effective policy requires coordination within the U.S. government. For the Congress, lobbying groups, prestige media, and others to play a constructive role, the executive must win their cooperation. The more that a Friendly Tyrants problem becomes headline news, the less control over policy the executive branch will retain; therefore, head off the emergence of dictatorial media celebrities.

Therefore,

- Honesty really is the best policy;
- Don't let foreign policy issues be captured by the wrong parts of the government;
- Beware the trap of multiple audiences;
- Do not ignore or abuse Congress;
- Discourage Congress from passing legislation or taking other initiatives to pressure Friendly Tyrants. . .
- . . .But if Congress does intrude, try to make the best of it by using it;
- Learn the proper care and feeding of the press, for even a hostile journalist has business interests;
- Remind the Friendly Tyrant you would preserve that "out of sight is out of mind";
- Do not indulge in post hoc acrimony when a Friendly Tyrants crisis goes awry, for this hinders future effectiveness.

9. Hedge Bets

Assume a gap between expectations and the actual power of U.S. policy to influence outcomes. Hedge bets by planning a healthy margin for error into every strategy.

Therefore,

• Do not assume the United States is central to a Friendly Tyrants crisis outcome;
• Remember that — short of a U.S. invasion — local forces decide political struggles;
• Do not assume that the sheer size of the United States guarantees success . . .
• . . .But remember that the U.S. government is usually perceived as more powerful than it is;
• Do not engage the office or the person of the president in a Friendly Tyrants episode unless a favorable outcome is certain; and
• If you resort to force to either preserve or topple a Friendly Tyrant, make sure that force is decisive.

10. Plan for Crises

Do not try to predict crises but do plan for them. Be ready for questions about what has happened, and prepare options for U.S. policy.

Therefore,

• Assume that a crisis will occur tomorrow morning, but don't cry wolf;

• Head off the emergence of tyrannical celebrities if you can, or any ensuing crisis will defy professional management;

• Make sure allies are included in your plans, and that their views are heard and understood before a crisis occurs;

• If the U.S. embassy staff is competent, play close attention to its information and views;

• Do not be seduced by classified information: the essence of what you need to know is in the newspaper;

• Be doubly wary of information that arrives through unorthodox channels;

• If the ousted tyrant takes refuge in the United States, do not prosecute him; and

• Do not lose interest once a Friendly Tyrant has left the scene, for another crisis may soon occur.

Appendix B: Pocket Chronologies

Pocket Chronologies

Argentina

1976-Humphrey-Kennedy amendment to the U.S. Foreign Assistance Act places preconditions on military aid, cutting arms shipments to Argentina.

March 1981-Reagan administration lifts military aid and training sanctions, renews support for Argentina at Export-Import bank and multilateral lending institutions; General Roberto Viola begins his term as president; Viola and General Leopoldo Galtieri are welcomed in Washington by President Reagan.

December 1981-General Leopoldo Galtieri replaces Viola as president and announces a plan to seize the Falkland Islands from the British.

March 1982-Esteban Takacs, Argentine ambassador to the United States, says the bilateral relationship between the two countries at "an optimal level"; large antigovernment demonstrations in Buenos Aires protest economic conditions.

April 1982-Argentine expeditionary force occupies Falkland Islands, and Secretary of State Haig tries to mediate a settlement.

April 28, 1982-Britain blockades the Falkland Islands, and shortly thereafter, a commando force is launched to seize control.

April 30, 1982-United States declares its support for Britain and rescinds military sales and trade privileges from Argentina.

June 14, 1982-Argentina surrenders to Britain.

June 17, 1982-General Galtieri resigns after the military loss and U.S. positions on the war are revealed to the Argentineans.

Cuba

March 1952-Mutual Defense Assistance Act between United States and Cuba limits arms use in Cuba to "hemispheric defense."

April 1952-Fulgenio Batista returns to power after seizing control of the military.

July 1953-Moncada Barracks army installation is attacked by a rebel force led by Fidel Castro; rebels are defeated.

1955-Batista grants an amnesty to Cuba's political prisoners.

November 1956-Castro leads guerrilla attack in Santiago, which is thwarted by Batista's forces.

March 1958-United States issues an embargo on arms to Cuba to facilitate Batista's removal.

April 1958-Castro declares "total war" on Batista regime, Batista suffers surprising losses.

June 1958-Castro's brother, Raul, hijacks a bus containing twenty-eight U.S. Marines and sailors; Castro releases them immediately after a strong U.S. reaction.

Fall 1958-Batista rigs elections.

December 1958-Castro's forces approach Havana after victories throughout Cuba.

January 1959-Batista flees Cuba and Castro assumes power.

February 1960-Cuba and the Soviet Union sign a crude oil trade agreement.

April 7, 1961-Bay of Pigs invasion pits CIA-backed Cuban exiles against Castro's forces and is a resounding failure.

1962-Castro forms Communist party in Cuba.

October 1962-Cuban missile crisis occurs.

Dominican Republic

1955-Vice President Nixon visits the Dominican Republic and the CIA establishes a base there.

December 1958-CIA offers aid to Dominicans who plotted the assassination of Rafael Trujillo.

1959-60-Rafael Trujillo asked to join American effort to isolate Castro

May 1960-President Eisenhower makes a contingency plan for a coup. against Trujillo

February 1960-William Pawley and Senator George Smathers are sent to request Trujillo's resignation.

1961-Triple coup in Dominican Republic, Haiti, and Cuba is planned.

January 1961-United States approves arms deliveries to Dominican dissidents.

May 1961-Trujillo assassinated in a CIA-linked conspiracy.

June 1961-Trujillo's son, Ramfis, assumes power, meets strong opposition.

November 1961-Ramfis and Trujillo family are exiled from Dominican Republic.

December 1962- Juan Bosch elected president; comes to Washington and confers with President Kennedy.

February 1963-Juan Bosch takes office.

April 1963-Military confrontation erupts between Dominican Republic and Haiti; U.S. controlled OAS panel begins mediation.

September 1963-Bosch overthrown in a coup.

April 1965-President Johnson orders U.S. Marines to stabilize military stalemate resulting from Bosch's attempted return to power.

Greece

1964-George Papandreou's Center Union party achieves plurality over Constantine Karamanlis's National Radical Union.

July 1965-United States pressures Center Union to side with King Constantine and Center Union collapses; congress dissolves and Papandreou resigns.

1965-66-United States formulates and updates the Prometheus plan to provide for a military takeover in Greece in the event of a national emergency.

April 14, 1967-Parliament dissolves again and the king threatens suspension of the constitution.

April 21, 1967-Greek colonels stage a successful coup lead by George Papadopolous; United States reacts mildly to the coup with no official denunciation.

December 1967-King feigns countercoup and flees to Rome.

January 1968-U.S. State Department praises junta's democratic initiatives, yet suspends shipments of heavy military equipment.

October 1968-Heavy military equipment shipments resumed.

January 1969-Nixon cuts delivery of heavy weapons again while maintaining smaller arms shipments.

1970-Secretary of Commerce Maurice Stans visits Greece and praises U.S.-Greek relations.

January 1971-State Department produces document brief of Greece, describing it as stable and moving toward democracy; Senate staffers write a scathing critique.

1972-Vice-President Spiro Agnew visits Greece, praises the regime.

June 1973-Martial law supposedly ends in Greece, and Greece is proclaimed a republic.

October 1973-Greece refuses to allow U.S. planes to refuel in Greece in order to resupply Israel in the October War.

July, 1974-Junta makes new plans for *enossis*, the merging of Cyprus with Greece, and plans a coup to overthrow Archbishop Makarios; Turkey invades Cyprus.

August 1974-Colonels' junta falls after United States fails to support Greece against Turkey, and Constantine Karamanlis forms a new post-junta government.

Fall 1974-Andreas Papandreou's leftist PASOK party wins power in free election and takes office.

Haiti

1957-François "Papa Doc" Duvalier takes control.

1963-United States accuses Duvalier of humans rights violations; aid is curtailed.

1964-François Duvalier becomes president-for-life.

1969-As U.S. presidential emissary, Nelson Rockefeller goes to Haiti.

1971-François Duvalier dies and is succeeded by Jean-Claude "Baby Doc" Duvalier.

1980-U.S.-Haitian relations are strained by the influx of Haitian refugee boat people into Florida, brought on by dire economic conditions in Haiti.

1981-Congress passes Mica Agreement, specifying human rights pre-conditions for foreign aid to Haiti; Duvalier tries to revitalize Haitian economy to gain U.S. support.

April 1982-Duvalier devises plans for free elections and a human rights commission.

July 1982-Key economic reformers in Duvalier's cabinet are dismissed, relations with the business community sour, yet U.S. aid levels are maintained..

November 1985-Antigovernment protesters clash with government security forces, inciting more riots throughout the country.

January 1986-United States suspends aid in response to street protests.

February 1986-"Baby Doc" is overthrown and flees Haiti aboard a U.S. cargo plane; Henri Namphy assumes leadership backed by substantial U.S. economic aid.

November 1987-U.S. aid to Namphy's corrupt government is cut.

January 1988-Namphy is replaced by Leslie Manigat in a semi-open election.

June 1988-Manigat fails to convince Washington to resume aid and his government falls.

November 1988-Planned elections are called off because of violence, General Prosper Avril comes to power.

March 1990-General Avril leaves Haiti aboard a U.S. plane.

Iran

1953-Coup backed by CIA and M-5 ousts Mossadegh and restores shah to power.

1969-Nixon's "Two Pillar" approach places Iran as a cornerstone of U.S. regional policy, large amounts of military and economic aid follow.

1972-President Nixon visits Teheran and promises shah access to any weapons system, save nuclear arms.

December 1977-Carter visits Iran and reiterates U.S. amity to the shah's government.

January 1978-Fundamentalist revolution begins.

December 1978-Khomeini-led fundamentalist revolution overthrows shah with surprising ease; Iranian crisis leads to second oil crisis, gas lines in the United States.

December 31, 1978-Carter administration shows support for Shahpour Bakhtiar's constitutional monarchist cabinet.

January 1979-Shah leaves Iran, enters United States; General Robert Huyser is sent to Iran to salvage U.S. military interests and support Bakhtiar's government.

February 1979-Fundamentalists gain full control.

November 1979-U.S. embassy in Teheran seized, U.S. hostages taken.

September 1980-Iran-Iraq war begins, U.S. interests jeopardized.

January 1981-U.S. hostages released.

Nicaragua

December 1974-FSLN raids house of José Maria Castillo Quant, inducing Somoza to make ransom payment and free imprisoned Sandinistas; Somoza declares "state of siege."

February 1976-Tomas Borge, a leader of the FSLN, is captured; FSLN insurgency is dampened by Somoza.

1976-Somoza's National Guard receives a generous U.S. aid package.

January 1978-Pedro Joaquín Chomorro, an opposition leader, is murdered.

August 1978-Sandinistas seize national palace in Managua.

September 1978-United States supports OAS mediation effort to force Somoza's resignation.

February 1979-United States terminates military assistance program and publicly denounces Somoza regime.

March 1979-FSLN fuses into one organization comprised of several opposition groups.

June-July 1979-Carter administration attempts to persuade FSLN to share power with moderates.

July 1979-Sandinistas seize full control.

October 1979-Carter donates money to Sandinistas that is eventually used in an El Salvadoran insurgency war.

February 1981- Reagan administration's "White Paper" blames Nicaragua and Cuba for communist infiltration in El Salvador.

Philippines

1972-Ferdinand Marcos declares martial law, U.S. response is mild.

1975-Trading and other economic sectors are centralized by a Marcos-led oligarchy.

1980-Secretary of State Edmund Muskie criticizes Marcos's undemocratic practices.

June 1981-Vice-President George Bush travels to Manila, praises Marcos after Philippino elections for his "devotion to democracy."

August 1983-Benigno (Ninoy) Aquino is murdered.

October 1983-U.S. ambassador Michael Armacost demands further investigation of Aquino's death.

January 1985-White House national security directive calls for increased pressure on Marcos for economic, political, and military reforms.

November 1985-Senator David Durenberger calls for Marcos to step down, Marcos announces early elections to avoid further U.S. criticism.

February 7, 1986-Corrupt elections occur.

February 16, 1986-Corazon Aquino calls for a nationwide strike in response to Marcos's fraudulent elections.

February 23, 1986-Philippine troops are sent to quell opposition, but later turn back or refuse to fight.

February 24, 1986-United States officially asks Marcos to step down.

February 25, 1986-Marcos and family flee Philippines aboard a U.S. plane to Hawaii, United States immediately recognizes the Aquino government.

1987-Racketeering charges are filed against Marcos in United States; Marcos dies.

South Vietnam

January 1960-Ngo Dinh Diem asks United States for increased military aid after Viet Cong engages ARVN troops.

1961-Kennedy steps up support after General Maxwell Taylor and Walt Rostow report on deteriorating situation in Vietnam.

1963-United States supports a coup against Diem; ARVN suffer numerous defeats.

1964-Tonkin Gulf incident occurs and President Johnson orders first U.S. air raids on North Vietnam.

1965-Combat Americanized.

1966-7-Viet Cong grows to a mass movement in response to increased U.S. involvement; General Westmoreland predicts victory to Congress.

February 1968-Tet offensive launched.

March 1968-Johnson halts bombing of North Vietnam and agrees to peace talks.

May 1969-Secret bombing of Cambodia is reported in *The New York Times*.

November 1969-Nixon announces "Vietnamization" policy troop withdrawal plan.

April 1970-Nixon orders invasion of Cambodia; antiwar demonstrations in the United States peak with Kent State shootings.

June 1971-After *The New York Times* begins publication of the Pentagon papers, Nixon orders the break-in of Daniel Ellsberg's office.

1972-Nixon reveals secret negotiations between Kissinger and North Vietnamese officials.

January 1973-Paris Accords signed, calling for a cease-fire while North Vietnamese troops are still in the South.

March 1973-Last U.S. troops are withdrawn.

1974-War Powers and Budget Reform Acts are passed, restricting the executive branch prerogative in foreign policy.

1974-75-Congress refuses sale of weapons to South Vietnam and Saigon falls to North Vietnam.

Index